HANDICRAFT SERIES (continued).

Glass Working by Heat and Abrasion. With 300 Engravings and Diagrams.

Contents.—Appliances used in Glass Blowing. Manipulating Glass Tubing. Blowing Bulbs and Flasks. Jointing Tubes to Bulbs forming Thistle Funnels, etc. Blowing and Etching Glass Fancy Articles; Embossing and Gilding Flat Surfaces. Utilising Broken Glass Apparatus; Boring Holes in, and Riveting Glass. Hand-working of Telescope Specula. Turning, Chipping, and Grinding Glass. The Manufacture of Glass.

Building Model Boats. With 168 Engravings and Diagrams.

Contents.—Building Model Yachts. Rigging and Sailing Model Yachts. Making and Fitting Simple Model Boats. Building a Model Atlantic Liner. Vertical Engine for a Model Launch. Model Launch Engine with Reversing Gear. Making a Show Case for a Model Boat.

Electric Bells, How to Make and Fit Them. With 162 Engravings and Diagrams.

Contents.—The Electric Current and the Laws that Govern it. Current Conductors used in Electric-Bell Work. Wiring for Electric Bells. Elaborated Systems of Wiring; Burglar Alarms. Batteries for Electric Bells. The Construction of Electric Bells, Pushes, and Switches. Indicators for Electric-Bell Systems.

Bamboo Work. With 177 Engravings and Diagrams.

Contents.—Bamboo: Its Sources and Uses. How to Work Bamboo. Bamboo Tables. Bamboo Chairs and Seats. Bamboo Bedroom Furniture. Bamboo Hall Racks and Stands. Bamboo Music Racks. Bamboo Cabinets and Bookcases. Bamboo Window Blinds. Miscellaneous Articles of Bamboo. Bamboo Mail Cart.

Taxidermy. With 108 Engravings and Diagrams.

Contents.—Skinning Birds. Stuffing and Mounting Birds. Skinning and Stuffing Mammals. Mounting Animals' Horned Heads: Polishing and Mounting Horns. Skinning, Stuffing, and Casting Fish. Preserving, Cleaning, and Dyeing Skins. Preserving Insects, and Birds' Eggs. Cases for Mounting Specimens.

Tailoring. With 180 Engravings and Diagrams.

Contents.—Tailors' Requisites and Methods of Stitching. Simple Repairs and Pressing. Relining, Repocketing, and Recollaring. How to Cut and Make Trousers. How to Cut and Make Vests. Cutting and Making Lounge and Reefer Jackets. Cutting and Making Morning and Frock Coats.

Photographic Cameras and Accessories. Comprising How to Make Cameras, Dark Slides, Shutters, and Stands. With 160 Illustrations.

Contents.—Photographic Lenses and How to Test them. Modern Half-plate Cameras. Hand and Pocket Cameras. Ferrotype Cameras. Stereoscopic Cameras. Enlarging Cameras. Dark Slides. Cinematograph Management.

Optical Lanterns. Comprising The Construction and Management of Optical Lanterns and the Making of Slides. With 160 Illustrations.

Contents.—Single Lanterns. Dissolving View Lanterns. Illuminant for Optical Lanterns. Optical Lantern Accessories. Conducting a Limelight Lantern Exhibition. Experiments with Optical Lanterns. Painting Lantern Slides. Photographic Lantern Slides. Mechanical Lantern Slides. Cinematograph Management.

Engraving Metals. With Numerous Illustrations.

Contents.—Introduction and Terms used. Engravers' Tools and their Uses. Elementary Exercises in Engraving. Engraving Plate and Precious Metals. Engraving Monograms. Transfer Processes of Engraving Metals. Engraving Name Plates. Engraving Coffin Plates. Engraving Steel Plates. Chasing and Embossing Metals. Etching Metals.

Basket Work. With 189 Illustrations.

Contents.—Tools and Materials. Simple Baskets. Grocer's Square Baskets. Round Baskets. Oval Baskets. Flat Fruit Baskets. Wicker Elbow Chairs. Basket Bottle-casings. Doctors' and Chemists' Baskets. Fancy Basket Work. Sussex Trug Basket. Miscellaneous Basket Work. Index

DAVID McKAY, Publisher, 610 South Washington Square, Philadelphia.

HANDICRAFT SERIES (continued).

Bookbinding. With 125 Engravings and Diagrams.
Contents.—Bookbinders' Appliances. Folding Printed Book Sheets. Beating and Sewing. Rounding, Backing, and Cover Cutting. Cutting Book Edges. Covering Books. Cloth-bound Books, Pamphlets, etc. Account Books, Ledgers, etc. Coloring, Sprinkling, and Marbling Book Edges. Marbling Book Papers. Gilding Book Edges. Sprinkling and Tree Marbling Book Covers. Lettering, Gilding, and Finishing Book Covers. Index.

Bent Iron Work. Including ELEMENTARY ART METAL WORK. With 269 Engravings and Diagrams.
Contents.—Tools and Materials. Bending and Working Strip Iron. Simple Exercises in Bent Iron. Floral Ornaments for Bent Iron Work. Candlesticks. Hall Lanterns. Screens, Grilles, etc. Table Lamps. Suspended Lamps and Flower Bowls. Photograph Frames. Newspaper Rack. Floor Lamps. Miscellaneous Examples. Index.

Photography. With 70 Engravings and Diagrams.
Contents.—The Camera and its Accessories. The Studio and Darkroom. Plates. Exposure. Developing and Fixing Negatives. Intensification and Reduction of Negatives. Portraiture and Picture Composition. Flashlight Photography. Retouching Negatives. Processes of Printing from Negatives. Mounting and Finishing Prints. Copying and Enlarging. Stereoscopic Photography. Ferrotype Photography. Index.

Upholstery. With 162 Engravings and Diagrams.
Contents.—Upholsterers' Materials. Upholsterers' Tools and Appliances. Webbing, Springing, Stuffing, and Tufting. Making Seat Cushions and Squabs. Upholstering an Easy Chair. Upholstering Couches and Sofas. Upholstering Footstools, Fenderettes, etc. Miscellaneous Upholstery. Mattress Making and Repairing. Fancy Upholstery. Renovating and Repairing Upholstered Furniture. Planning and Laying Carpets and Linoleum. Index.

Leather Working. With 152 Engravings and Diagrams.
Contents.—Qualities and Varieties of Leather. Strap Cutting and Making. Letter Cases and Writing Pads. Hair Brush and Collar Cases. Hat Cases. Banjo and Mandoline Cases. Bags. Portmanteaux and Travelling Trunks. Knapsacks and Satchels. Leather Ornamentation. Footballs. Dyeing Leather. Miscellaneous Examples of Leather Work. Index.

Harness Making. With 197 Engravings and Diagrams.
Contents.—Harness Makers' Tools. Harness Makers' Materials. Simple Exercises in Stitching. Looping. Cart Harness. Cart Collars. Cart Saddles. Fore Gear and Leader Harness. Plough Harness. Bits, Spurs, Stirrups, and Harness Furniture. Van and Cab Harness. Index.

Saddlery. With 99 Engravings and Diagrams.
Contents.—Gentleman's Riding Saddle. Panel for Gentleman's Saddle. Ladies' Side Saddles. Children's Saddles or Pilches. Saddle Cruppers, Breastplates, and other Accessories. Riding Bridles. Breaking-down Tackle. Head Collars. Horse Clothing. Knee-caps and Miscellaneous Articles. Repairing Harness and Saddlery. Re-lining Collars and Saddles. Riding and Driving Whips. Superior Set of Gig Harness. Index.

Knotting and Splicing, Ropes and Cordage. With 208 Engravings and Diagrams.
Contents.—Introduction. Rope Formation. Simple and Useful Knots. Eye Knots, Hitches and Bends. Ring Knots and Rope Shortenings. Ties and Lashings. Fancy Knots. Rope Splicing. Working Cordage. Hammock Making. Lashings and Ties for Scaffolding. Splicing and Socketing Wire Ropes. Index.

Beehives and Beekeepers' Appliances. With 155 Engravings and Diagrams.
Contents.—Introduction. A Bar-Frame Beehive. Temporary Beehive. Tiering Bar-Frame Beehive. The "W. B. C." Beehive. Furnishing and Stocking a Beehive. Observatory Beehive for Permanent Use. Observatory Beehive for Temporary Use. Inspection Case for Beehives. Hive for Rearing Queen Bees. Super-Clearers. Bee Smoker. Honey Extractors. Wax Extractors. Beekeepers' Miscellaneous Appliances. Index.

DAVID McKAY, Publisher, 610 South Washington Square, Philadelphia.

BASKET WORK
OF ALL KINDS

With Numerous Engravings and Diagrams

EDITED BY
PAUL N. HASLUCK

Author of "Handybooks for Handicrafts," etc. etc.

PHILADELPHIA
DAVID McKAY, Publisher
610, *SOUTH WASHINGTON SQUARE*
1911

PREFACE

THIS Handbook contains, in form convenient for everyday use, a comprehensive digest of the knowledge of basket work of all kinds, scattered over more than twenty thousand columns of WORK—one of the weekly journals it is my fortune to edit—and supplies concise information on the details of the subject of which it treats.

In preparing for publication in book form the mass of relevant matter contained in the volumes of WORK, some had to be arranged anew, altered, and largely re-written. However, it may be stated that the greater part of the contents of this Handbook consists substantially of matter contributed by a working basket maker.

Readers who may desire additional information respecting special details of the matters dealt with in this Handbook, or instructions on kindred subjects, should address a question to WORK, so that it may be answered in the columns of that journal.

P. N. HASLUCK.

La Belle Sauvage, London.

CONTENTS

CHAP.	PAGE
I.—Tools and Materials	9
II.—Simple Baskets	16
III.—Grocers' Square Baskets	27
IV.—Round Baskets	49
V.—Oval Baskets	55
VI.—Flat Fruit Baskets	64
VII.—Wicker Elbow-chairs	74
VIII.—Basket Bottle-casings	98
IX.—Doctors' and Chemists' Baskets	104
X.—Fancy Baskets	112
XI.—Sussex Trug Baskets	132
XII.—Miscellaneous Basket Work	147
Index	157

LIST OF ILLUSTRATIONS

FIG.		PAGE
1.—Screw-block	. . .	10
2.—Commander	. . .	10
3.—Picking Knife	. . .	11
4.—Shop Knife	. . .	11
5.—Small Bodkin	. . .	11
6.—Large Bodkin	. . .	11
7.—Shears	. . .	11
8.—Flat Iron	. . .	12
9.—Yard Stick	. . .	12
10.—Cleave for Peeling Osiers		12
11.—Cleave Iron	. . .	12
12-15.—Cleaves for Splitting Osiers		13
16, 17.—Shave	. . .	13
18, 19.—Upright Shave	. .	14
20.—Awl	. . .	14
21.—Simple Round Basket	.	17
22.—Beginning Round Basket	.	17
23.—Foundation for Round Basket		18
24.—Method of Joining	. .	19
25.—Twist	. . .	20
26.—Trellis Edge	. . .	21
27.—Simple Beginning for Basket		22
28.—Plaited Beginning for Basket		22
29.—Beginning Oval Basket	.	23
30.—Finished Rope Edge	. .	24
31.—Rope Edge: First Stage	.	25
32.—Rope Edge: Second Stage	.	26
33.—Basket Bottom in Screw-block		29
34.—Simple Weaving	. .	31
35.—Hooping Stakes	. .	33
36.—Staking Basket Bottom	.	33
37.—Corner Stick	. . .	33
38.—Upsetting Sides of Basket	.	35
39.—Fixing Corner Stick	. .	36
40.—Piecing in Upsetting	. .	36
41.—Weaving Sides of Basket	.	39
42.—Strainer	. . .	41
43.—Waling	. . .	41
44.—Waling round Corner Sticks		44
45.—Side View of Bordering	.	44
46.—Top View of Bordering	.	44
47.—Cramming	. . .	44
48.—Bow for Basket	. .	47
49.—Bordering Foot Rim	. .	47
50, 51.—Lapping Handle Bow	.	47
52.—Round Slarth	. . .	50
53.—Working Tie-rods together	.	50
54.—Bottom of Round Basket	.	51
55.—Filling in Stakes	. .	52
56.—Border for Round Basket	.	53
57.—Oval Slarth	. . .	56
58.—Slarth Rods in Position	.	56

FIG.		PAGE
59.—Tying Slarth	. . .	57
60.—Opening Bottom Sticks	.	59
61.—Siding up Oval Linen Basket		60
62.—Bordering Oval Linen Basket		61
63.—Handle of Oval Linen Basket		62
64.—Turning Back Rod in making Handle		63
65.—Beginning Flat Basket	.	65
66.—Handle of Flat Basket	.	67
67.—Bordering Corner of Flat Basket		68
68.—Bow and Scallom Rods	.	68
69.—Beginning Basket Lid	.	69
70.—Front of Basket Lid	.	71
71.—Piecing Bow	. . .	71
72.—Finishing Basket Lid	.	72
73.—Tying on Basket Lid	.	73
74.—Wicker Elbow-chair	. .	75
75.—Lapping Scallops on Bow	.	76
76.—Cut Butt End	. . .	76
77.—Weaving Chair Seat	. .	77
78.—Working Sticks in Upsetting		78
79.—Staking Chair Seat	. .	78
80.—Upsetting Foot of Chair	.	79
81.—Fetching	. . .	80
82.—Bending Tops of Fetch-rods		80
83.—Piecing Rod	. . .	80
84.—Piecing Fetching	. .	81
85.—Fetches in Foot of Chair	.	82
86.—Bordering of Foot of Chair	.	83
87.—Bordering Round Chair Corner Post		84
88.—Finishing Bordering	. .	85
89.—Cramming Down Stakes	.	85
90.—Bordering at Edge of Chair Seat		86
91.—Finishing Bordering	. .	87
92.—Beginning Fetching	. .	88
93.—Working Pair of Rods on Fetch-rods		89
94.—Beginning Second Fetch on Chair Back		90
95.—Crossing Stakes in Fetching	91
96.—Plaiting Border	. .	92
97.—Bending Stakes in Plaited Border		93
98.—Splitting End of Rod	.	94
99.—Inserting Cleave in Rod	.	95
100.—Finishing-off Chair Post	.	96
101.—Beginning Cap of Bottle-casing		99
102.—Working Strand round Bottle Neck		99

FIG.	PAGE
103.—Plan of Cap of Casing	100
104.—Part of Casing, showing Tap Opening	101
105.—Scallomed Rod	101
106.—Border on Bottle-casing	102
107.—Handle on Bottle-casing	102
108.—Bordering Doctor's Basket	105
109, 110.—Working Bridge for Doctor's Basket	107
111.—Flap Lid for Doctor's Basket	107
112.—Scallom Rod	109
113.—Finishing Lid	109
114–118.—Forming Bands for Doctor's Basket	109, 111
119, 120.—Lapping Handle	111
121.—Piecing Skeins	111
122.—Staple	111
123.—Open-work Design	113
124.—Spoke and Twist Design	114
125.—Crossed Open-work Design	114
126.—Zigzag Pattern	115
127.—Sewing	116
128, 129.—Basket Frame	117
130.—Bottom of Oblong Basket	118
131.—Square Fancy Basket	118
132.—Weaving Square Fancy Basket	121
133.—Handle for Fancy Basket	122
134.—Doll's Garden Chair	123
135.—Doll's Round Chair	123
136.—Doll's Cradle	124
137.—Hood of Cradle	125
138.—Doll's Table	125
139–141.—Constructing Doll's Table	125
142.—Fire-screen	126
143.—Basket Work of Screen	126
144.—Screen Stand	126
145.—Paper Rack	127
146, 147.—Constructing Paper Rack	128
148.—Handle of Paper Rack	128

FIG.	PAGE
149.—Open-work Side for Paper Rack	128
150.—Doll's Bedstead	130
151.—Madeira Open-work Basket	130
152.—Side of Madeira Basket	131
153, 154.—Shaving-horse	133
155, 156.—Shaving-brake	134
157.—Steaming Trough	135
158.—Steaming Apparatus	136
159, 160.—End of Steam Trough	136
161.—Attachment of Steam Tube to Copper	136
162, 163.—Sussex Trug	137
164.—Rim of Sussex Trug	138
165.—Handle of Sussex Trug	138
166.—Foot of Sussex Trug	138
167.—Boards of Sussex Trug	139
168, 169.—Sections of Rim of Sussex Trug	139
170.—Cleaving Axe	142
171.—Walking-stick Basket	142
172.—Collar of Walking-stick Basket	142
173.—Caul or Wood Basket	142
174.—Stable or Feeding Basket	143
175.—Coal Basket	143
176, 177.—Lady's Work Basket	144, 145
178.—Handles for Work Baskets	146
179.—Weaving for Hawker's Basket	148
180.—Waling for Hawker's Basket	148
181.—Basket for Show Fowls	149
182.—Woven Twisted Rods	150
183.—Eel Trap	150
184.—Crab and Lobster Pot	151
185.—Border for Single-stick Hand-guard	153
186.—Tying-in Band	153
187.—Bottom of Strawberry Punnet	154
188, 189.—Uprights and Lacing of Strawberry Punnet	155

BASKET WORK

CHAPTER I.

TOOLS AND MATERIALS.

BASKET work is so easily done and at such a small cost that almost anyone can practise it. No patterns require to be drawn, and but very few tools are necessary; and some charming presents or really useful and saleable articles can be made for the most trifling expense.

First of all, the tools required will be described. Fig. 1, p.10, shows one end of a screw-block, in which all square baskets and wicker elbow chairs are begun. Two lengths of wood, each 3 ft. 2 in. long, 2½ in. thick, and 3 in. wide, are required. The best wood to use is well seasoned oak, but, of course, common deal can be used, but the harder the wood the better. At 6½ in. from each end bore ½-in. holes for bolts 8 in. long, the nuts for which have a bow as illustrated in Fig. 1. The bolts may have square shoulders let in the block to prevent them turning when screwing up. Any smith will make these bolts. Bore the holes through the 2½ in. way of the stuff.

Fig. 2 shows a tool known as a commander; this is made of iron ½ in. thick, with two rings, one at each end, and respectively of 1½ in. and 2 in. inside diameter. The commander is used for straightening thick bent sticks, but is not often required. Fig. 3, p. 11, shows a picking or trimming knife, and Fig. 4 a general shop knife. Figs. 5 and 6 show small and large bodkins respectively; these are driven through sticks, etc., to make a way for pushing in stakes. Fig. 7 shows a pair of shears for cutting osiers; they must be strong, and about 10 in. or 12 in. long. Fig. 8, p. 12, shows a flat iron, which is used with the bodkins, also to drive the osiers close together. A yard measure is also required; this is best made from a brown osier, that is, one with peel on, as then it is easily distinguished from the white osiers lying about. Make a notch at every inch and cross the notch at every 6 in., as indicated by Fig. 9, p. 12.

Osiers of different sizes for basket-making can be bought in most towns by weight or by the bolt or

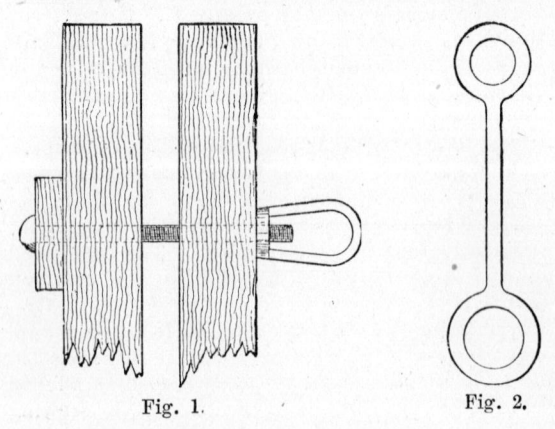

Fig. 1.   Fig. 2.

Fig. 1.—Screw-block; Fig. 2.—Commander.

bundle. For peeling them, a cleave, shaped as Fig. 10, is used; this is a well-seasoned stake of wood, about 3 ft. long, and 3 in. thick at the thickest part. Some of its heart is removed with a saw, commencing at the thinnest end, for about 18 in. of its length; this piece is then cut out with a sharp chisel to the shape shown at A. Two pieces of triangular-shaped iron D (shown in section, Fig. 11) then are secured with screws to B and C, the slightly rounded angle of each exactly facing the other. When B and c are pressed together with the left hand, and the osier pulled between the two irons, the peel is

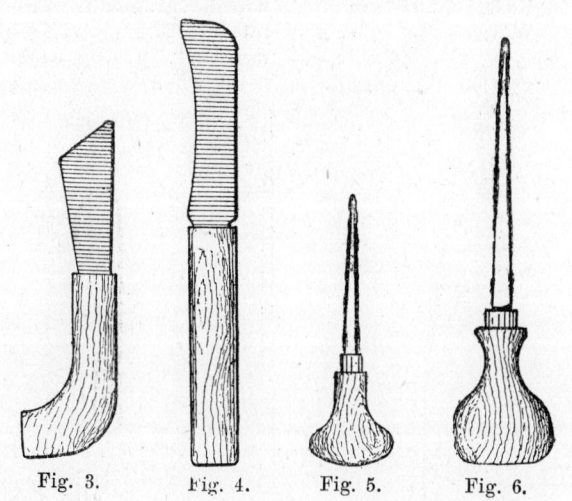

Fig. 3.   Fig. 4.   Fig. 5.   Fig. 6.

Fig. 3.—Picking Knife; Fig. 4.—Shop Knife; Fig. 5.—Small Bodkin; Fig. 6.—Large Bodkin.

riven in two and easily removed, without in any way injuring the white heart of the osier.

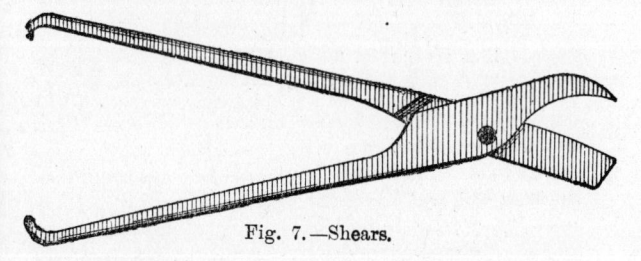

Fig. 7.—Shears.

To make osiers workable, they must be damped in bundles, either by sprinkling from the rose of a water-can, or by dipping them in a long trough containing water, and laying them on some clean damp surface, and covering them with damp sacking; anyhow, the water must penetrate the osiers, and then they will be pliable and workable. If the water hangs on the outside of them when commencing

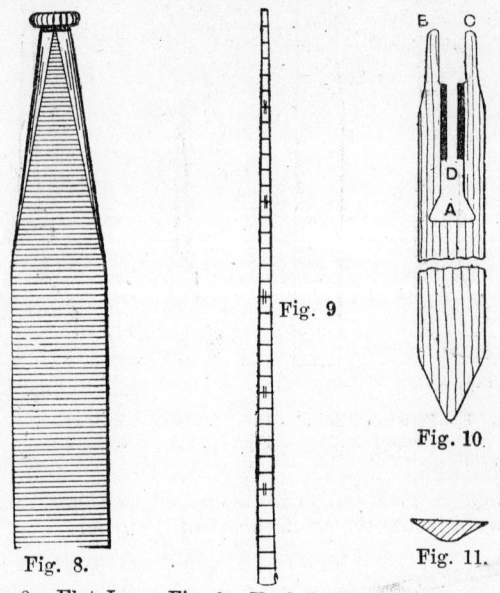

Fig. 8.

Fig. 9.

Fig. 10.

Fig. 11.

Fig. 8.—Flat Iron; Fig. 9.—Yard Stick; Fig. 10.—Cleave for Peeling Osiers; Fig. 11.—Cleave Iron.

work, stand them separate on their top ends for a few minutes, when the water will drain off quickly. Brown osiers take some time to soak to get them into working order; fresh-cut, green osiers are never used; they have to be left for several months to get thoroughly shrunk and dry. These osiers ought to lie in a trough of water for several days; failing this, they must be laid close together in bundles, well watered occasionally, and covered with wet sacking. If wanted quickly, boiling water might be tried. Almost any osiers, even those of inferior quality, can be made serviceable by boiling them. By handling one or two of the rods occasionally the workman can easily tell when they are in a workable condition.

The fashionable buff-coloured chairs are made from osiers that have been boiled with the peel on. The peel or bark stains the white heart of the rod

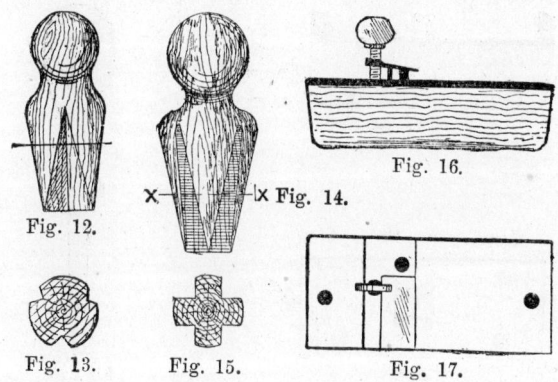

Fig. 12. Fig. 14. Fig. 16.

Fig. 13. Fig. 15. Fig. 17.

Figs. 12 to 16.—Cleaves for Splitting Osiers; Figs. 16 and 17.—Shave.

permanently. The skins are stripped off, after which the buff osiers are dried thoroughly in the open air. These buff osiers can be bought, but they are more expensive than white ones.

For making skeins from osiers, several further tools are required. Skeins are used for making chaff sieves, for finishing some chairs, mending, etc. A boxwood cleave or two (Figs. 12 to 15) will be needed, one to split the rods into three (Figs. 12 and 13), another (Figs. 14 and 15) to split larger rods into four; the shave (Figs. 16 and 17) is employed for removing the pith from the skeins and is held in the left hand, against the left knee. The top end of the skein is put in between the iron plate and the fixed knife, and then pulled through with the right hand. A leather thumb-cot will have to be made; this is slipped on the left thumb, which presses the skein against the iron plate, close to the knife. If the knife is in good order and the shave held firmly, a shaving can be taken off from end to end. Another tool, the upright shave (Figs. 18 and 19) is for reducing the skeins to the same width from end to end,

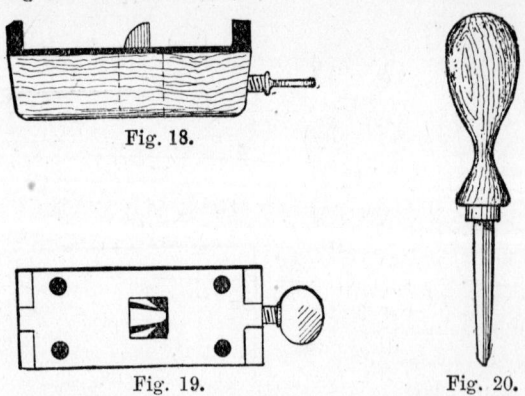

Fig. 18.

Fig. 19.   Fig. 20.

Figs. 18 and 19.—Upright Shave; Fig. 20.—Awl.

the butt end of a rod being much thicker than the top end. The basketmaker's awl is illustrated by Fig. 20. Two work-boards will be required, one to sit on, and the other for the work to rest on. To make such a board, take an 11-in. plank, about ¾ in. thick, saw off two 3 ft. 6 in. pieces for each board, and nail the ends to pieces 22 in. long, 4 in. wide, and 1½ in. thick. The boards will then be 22 in. wide and raised 4 in. from the ground. By using these boards the workman has complete control over the work; he sits at one end, his legs projecting one each side, and the work-board rests upon his knees, or, what is more pleasant, upon a small loose block of wood a little thicker than his legs. As the work proceeds the workman will have to raise himself, and a higher seat will be required.

For fancy basket work, reeds and canes are used, and in the event of it being desired to bleach the canes, chloride of lime is employed. First dissolve about 1 lb. of washing soda in 1 gal. of water, and, while it is still warm, steep the canes in it for an hour or two. Remove, and steep in clean water. Next prepare a solution of chloride of lime, 1 lb. to 2 gal. of water; allow the canes to steep in this overnight, remove, and place in a bath of dilute sulphuric acid, 1 part of acid to 12 parts of water; remove again, and wash for several hours in running water to remove the acid. Try the above method on samples of the cane first.

Several kinds of stains and varnishes are used for baskets. Most stains are applied after the baskets are made. Brown japan thinned with turpentine will give a mahogany colour. See that the baskets are thoroughly dry, then give a coat of the japan applied with a brush. When dry, give a second, but somewhat thicker, coat.

A brown stain for basket work is made with permanganate of potash, 1 oz. to one quart of water. Then apply a second stain consisting of ¼ lb. of American brown potash, 1 oz. of nut-galls, and 3 qt. of water. Colour to the tone desired with vandyke brown.

A method of imparting a mahogany colour is to coat the baskets with a solution of gum in water. When dry, brush over some bichromate of potash dissolved in hot water. Finally, give a coat of shellac varnish. Still another method is to boil some logwood chips, or extract, in water, then carefully add some sulphuric acid: this can be either poured over or brushed on the baskets. Finish by varnishing as before. Any good varnish is suitable.

CHAPTER II.

SIMPLE BASKETS.

THE elements of basket work can be learnt by using thin cane, which is managed more easily than osiers are. For weaving the sides of the little basket shown by Fig. 21, obtain one bundle of No. 3 cane, and for the uprights or radials one bundle of No. 8 canes; the uprights ought to be thicker than the weaving.

Cut a sufficient number of pieces of the thick cane for the radials of the bottom which also form the uprights of the sides, which must be long enough to go down one side of the basket, across the bottom, and up the other side, besides an extra length of 8 in. or 10 in. to make an ornamental edge round the top of the basket.

For a first attempt, a basket 4 in. or 5 in. high and 5 in. across the bottom will answer; therefore the radials must each be about 30 in. long. The more stakes there are, the firmer the basket will be; but for this size eight will be enough, each 30 in. long, and one piece half that length (15 in.). Soak them in water (hot or cold) for about twenty minutes, together with a dozen lengths of the No. 3 cane. Do not cut up the thin cane, as it is an advantage to have it in long lengths for weaving, to avoid joins. When sufficiently soaked, lay four radials side by side, holding them in the middle with the left hand, and place the other four pieces across them at right angles, crossing in the middle, with the extra short piece inserted only as far as the middle of the crossing, as shown in Fig. 22. Hold the pieces in position with the left hand, and with a long length

SIMPLE BASKETS. 17

of the No. 3 cane fasten them tightly together. The easiest way of doing this is to push in one end of the thin cane between the two sets of radials, and wind

Fig. 21.—Simple Round Basket.

it firmly round and round to hold them all in their places—thus: push in the end at the corner marked A (Fig. 22), then bring the weaving piece over all the pieces marked B, under all those at C, over D, and

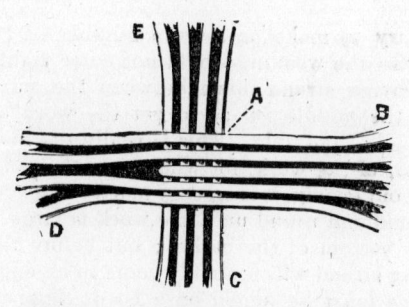

Fig. 22.—Beginning Round Basket.

under E. This should be done three times round, and will keep them all together, as in Fig. 23. This crossing place will be the middle of the bottom of

B

the basket, and if this middle is not tightly fastened the whole basket will be loose and unsteady, so that it is important to pull the tying strand as tightly as possible.

Begin now to pull the radials apart, and continue weaving with the same long strand, only over and under each cane alternately. Hold the tied part in the left hand, and weave in and out with the right hand, turning the work round and round. After a few rounds the radials ought to stand out at even distances, resembling a spider's web. Observe that the half-cane, put in only as far as the middle, is

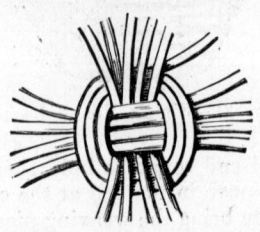

Fig. 23.—Foundation for Round Basket.

necessary to make an uneven number of radials; otherwise the weaving would not come right. Pull the weaving strand down between the radials towards the middle, so as to get the work as tight and close as possible. This is really the most difficult part of the work, for when once the radials are spread out evenly, it is an easy matter to go on weaving round and round until the work is large enough for the bottom of the basket; but before that the weaving strand will probably come to an end, and a new one must be joined on. To do this, work to the end of the first strand, and then begin the new one four or five radials further back by pushing in one end between the old strand and one of the radials (as shown in Fig. 24), and weave the two together—not one over the other, as that would make an extra row just there, but one in front of the other —till the old strand comes to an end and the new one is ready to go on with. This ought to make an almost imperceptible join, but sometimes one end will poke out, in spite of every care. If so, leave it alone till the basket is finished, and when dry cut it off.

When the bottom of the basket is 5 in. in diameter, the radials must be turned up to make the uprights of the sides. The piece already made will probably not be flat; but this is all the better, as the basket will stand more steadily if the bottom is a little raised in the middle. Therefore, stand it on a table with the hollow side downwards, and

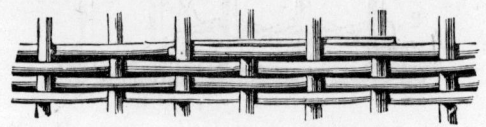

Fig. 24.—Method of Joining.

bend up each spoke in turn. It is a good plan to put the whole thing in water again for a few minutes before doing this, so as to make it quite soft and pliable, for if too dry the radials will crack instead of bending. A slight crack does not much matter, but if a radial really breaks off, it must be cut as short as possible, and a new one pushed in by the side of it as far as the middle; but with ordinary care the rods will not break, for if they are damp enough they can be bent up quite close to the last row of weaving. They will not stay upright till after a few rows of weaving have been done.

The best plan is to rest the work edgeways on a table or on the knee, with the uprights pointing away from the worker, and weave round and round as before from left to right, only pulling the strand tight to make the uprights stand upright, which they will very soon do. The shape will be improved greatly if the sides can be sloped a little outwards, but it needs practice to do this evenly all round. It is a great help to put a basin or flower-pot inside the basket and work it round, though it is best to learn to do without such help. Always press down each row of weaving as it is completed, to make the basket firm, the left hand pressing down the weaving while the right holds the weaving strand.

When the sides of the basket are 5 in. high (or whatever height seems a good proportion), the edge may be finished off. Take a short piece of No. 3 cane, rather longer than the circumference of the

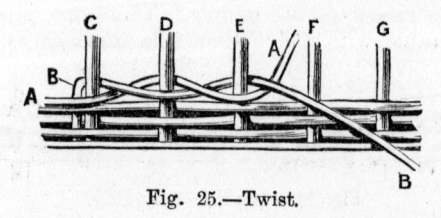

Fig. 25.—Twist.

basket, and push one end behind the weaving strand, as if for a join—or else push the end down by the side of the last upright—and then make a twist of the two strands, using them alternately—thus: Take the new strand B (Fig. 25) behind upright C and in front of D; while the old strand A goes in front of C and behind D. Then B goes behind E, A goes behind F, B goes behind G, and so on all round. This makes a neat twist, firmer than ordinary weaving, and prevents the top row coming undone. When round to the beginning of the twist, cut off both of the strands, leaving ends about 1 in. long, and push these ends down by the side of an upright, or wind them into the first loop of the twist, to fasten off. It may here be mentioned that a twist like this is a great improvement round the bottom of a basket before beginning to turn up the sides.

Now the basket is finished, but the tops of the uprights remain to be disposed of. For a beginner the easiest plan is a trellis-work edging executed as follows: Bend over one of the stakes, as in Fig. 26, and measure the height of the basket; cut it off at A, and, after pasing it behind B, push it down carefully between the weaving strands, close by the side of upright C, that being the next upright but one. Then cut B in the same way, bend it behind

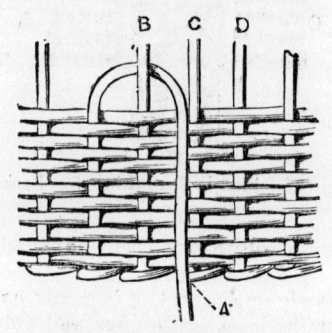

Fig. 26.—Trellis Edge.

C, and push it down by the side of D. For this pushing down a tool is a great help to make an opening between the strands for the spoke to pass. It can be done with scissors or with a common skewer, but the bodkin (see p. 11) is the most convenient.

Care must be taken to make the edging the same height all the way round the basket. When the basket is finished and still damp a good deal of shaping can be done, if necessary, by judicious pinching, damping it again if required. The bottom may need to be pushed up to make it stand steadily, or one part will be found to slope out more than another. Shape it as well as it is possible, and then let it dry without touching it again, when it will become quite stiff and firm. When quite dry it should be looked over, and any ends cut off that may have poked out at the joins. The basket shrinks a little in drying, therefore the ends should

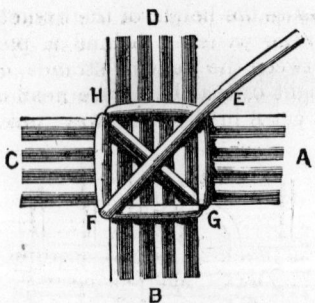

Fig. 27.—Simple Beginning for Basket.

not be cut till quite dry. The finished basket is illustrated by Fig. 21, p. 17.

Having made one basket, it becomes easy to learn different methods of beginnings and various kinds of edges.

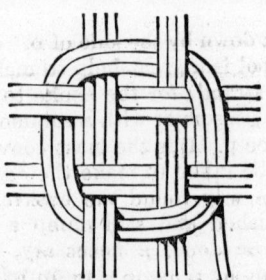

Fig. 28.—Plaited Beginning for Basket.

A very firm beginning is to cross the radials in the middle, poke in one end of the weaving strand as before, and then fasten it round the radials, as shown by Fig. 27. When done, it should be alike on both sides, with a cross from corner to corner and a straight tie on each side forming a square. It is of no consequence how this is done, but the following rule will help in bringing it right: Begin at the corner E (Fig. 27). Bring the strand under the radials A, over B, under C, over D; now across on the under side, from E to F, then round again, over C, under D, over A; cross underneath from G to H and back again over to G, under B, and over again from F to E. This finishes the tie, and the strand is ready to go under the first radial at A to begin the weaving.

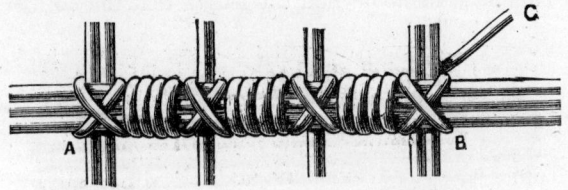

Fig. 29.—Beginning Oval Basket.

Another beginning is to divide, say, twelve radials into four equal bundles, lay them in a square interlacing each other, and wind round three or four times before beginning to divide the radials, as in Fig. 28. This is a pretty beginning, but it leaves a square hole at the bottom of the basket.

Sometimes it seems difficult to get the radials to spread evenly apart, especially if they are tied very tightly. One way to overcome this difficulty is to begin the weaving by going over two radials and under two alternately, instead of over and under one only. When back again to the beginning, if there is an uneven number of radials, the second round of weaving will divide the two radials that went together the first time, and after a few rounds it will be seen that this makes a very close kind of twisted weaving of good appearance. If about 3 in.

in diameter is worked like this, and then the rest in the ordinary weaving, over and under one only, it has a very good effect.

An oval basket must be begun in a different way. Lay three canes side by side for the long way of the basket, with two crosspieces above it; tie these with a cross-tie, then wind the tying strand round the long-way radials for about half an inch; lay on another crosspiece and fasten that; wind round again for another half-inch, lay another crosspiece, and so on until it is long enough, putting two crosspieces together the last time, as at the beginning (see Fig. 29). This must be about half the length that the bottom

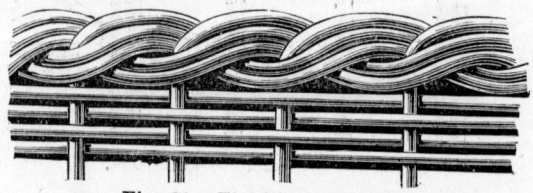

Fig. 30.—Finished Rope Edge.

is required to be—that is to say, if a basket 8 in. long is required, it must be 4 in. from A to B (Fig. 29). Then weave in and out as usual with the weaving strand C, pulling the end crosspieces apart; but as the even number of canes would bring the weaving wrong, either an odd cane must be put in at one end, which will make the basket uneven, or two strands must be used for weaving, which is better. In the second case, work all round with one strand, and when back again to the beginning leave the first strand hanging loose; take the second strand and work a row with that, then the first strand again, and so on alternately. The sides are to be turned up exactly the same as for a round basket, but ovals are much more difficult to shape evenly than round ones, though a little practice will soon bring it all right. Dolls' cradles can be made just like oval baskets, leaving the uprights extra long at one end to make the hood.

There are many different ways of finishing off the tops of baskets. One of the most useful is a thick rope edging (Fig. 30), for which the uprights must be quite 14 in. above the top of the basket, and they should be very damp.

For the rope edging, take any upright to begin with, A Fig. 31, bend it to the right in front of B, behind C, and then bend B down on the top of it. Take C in front of D, behind E, and bend D down upon it. There are now two pairs of bent-over

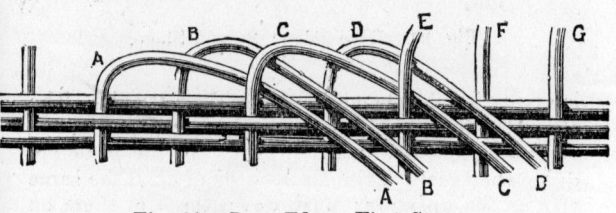

Fig. 31.—Rope Edge: First Stage.

spokes. Take the upper one of the left-hand pair, B, pass it in front of E, behind F, and bend E down upon it. Now there are again two pairs. Take the upper one of the left-hand pair as before (this time it will be D); repeat this all round. D will go in front of F, behind G, and F down upon it. When back again to the starting-place the first four spokes, A, B, C, and D, must be pulled out, as the beginning did not really follow the correct rule, and they must be pushed in and out, following the same rule as the rest, so that the twist is exactly alike all round. The edges should now resemble Fig. 32, with all the ends outside the basket. To finish the twist, take A (Fig. 32) and push it in at the opening B; take C and push it in at D, and so on all round, enlarging the opening, if required, with the bodkin. The ends will now be all inside the basket. Cut them off, leaving about an inch, and when the whole thing is quite dry cut them off quite close to the twist. If cut short before drying they are sure to shrink and fly out. This

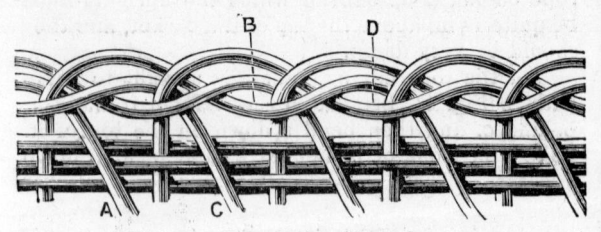

Fig. 32.—Rope Edge: Second Stage.

is a very handsome edging when done evenly. The closer the uprights the better it looks. (See Fig. 30.)

If a handle is wanted, it should be put in before doing the twist. Take six lengths of cane the same size as the uprights; push down three of them on one side of an upright and three on the other. Twist the two sets together, and push them down by the corresponding upright on the opposite side of the basket. The twist will hold them tight, or they can be tied as well if considered advisable.

CHAPTER III.

GROCERS' SQUARE BASKETS.

When success has been attained in the light cane basket-work described in the previous chapter, really practical and useful work with osiers may be attempted. The grocers' square basket about to be described has a bow handle over the open top, and in making it there will be great help in examining a basket of this type. Place the screw-block (Fig. 1, p. 10) on the working-board, one end of which should rest on the sitting-board. The basket is to have a bottom 17 in. long, is to be 11 in. wide, and 11 in. deep from the bottom to the wale, as the finishing-off just under the top border is called. With the shears (Fig. 7, p. 11) cut six sticks 20 in. long; the extra 3 in. is for fixing them in the screw-block and leaving a little to spare at the other end where the bottom is finished off. These sticks can be obtained where the osiers are purchased. An old basket would be useful to a beginner as a guide as to size or diameter of the sticks and stakes, as, indeed, it often is to an old hand. As a rough guide, however, the two outside sticks may be $\frac{3}{4}$ in. thick at the thickest end, and the four inside ones about $\frac{5}{8}$ in. Cut the thinnest ends of the two outside ones wedge shape, and tap them in the block with the iron, always with the bow or bent side of the sticks from the sitter; this applies to all sticks fixed in the block, as the stakes used afterwards have a tendency to draw the bottom upwards. These sticks will be better for being wetted and covered an hour before using; those that are too much bent can then be straightened without breaking. The basket maker should keep a bucketful of water at the left side, or somewhere near, with a sponge in it. After the two outside sticks are put in the block 11 in. apart, outside measure, screw the block up a trifle, just to grip them firmly, and put in the inside sticks at equal distances; all the thick ends will have to be cut wedge shape, and they are tapped in alternately, first a thick end, then a thin end, and so on as shown in Fig. 33. Now screw up tight, using the large bodkin in the bow-nuts to turn them round. Take a double handful of small osiers, place them on the floor at the right-hand side, and take two of the thickest and longest to begin filling up; place one of the butt-ends behind the left-hand outside stick, so that the extreme end projects a little beyond the inside front of the third stick; grip the butt and the second stick firmly, and with the left hand bring the osier round the outside stick, then behind the second, and leave it in front of the third stick. Now take the short butt-end, place it over that just worked, and lay it behind the third stick. Now take the second osier, lay its butt beside the last butt, and bring its top part in front of the fourth stick; now the first osier over the second, behind the fourth, and in front of the fifth stick; again the second osier behind the fifth stick and in front of the sixth or outside stick; then the first behind the sixth. Leave it there while carrying the second osier round the stick and underneath the first osier, pulling it tight in front of the fifth stick. Now the first osier is brought round the stick, behind the fifth stick, and left in front of the fourth stick, and so continue to work the two rods up. The worker will find the osiers strange to handle at first, but this feeling will soon wear off; and, by gripping them firmly, they will bend without kinks or breakage.

The reason for working the two rods or osiers together when beginning a bottom is that it prevents the after-weaving from becoming undone when the finished bottom is taken out of the screw-block. Now, with the yard measure and a pencil, mark off 17 in. on each outside stick; for width, take a small straight rod, and at 11 in. from the butt-end bend it at right angles, and tie the top end in a loop to distinguish it from the rest; this must be used every few inches as the work proceeds, because the weaving has a tendency to draw the outside sticks inwards. Every time the rod is brought round the outside sticks clasp the first inside sticks, and with

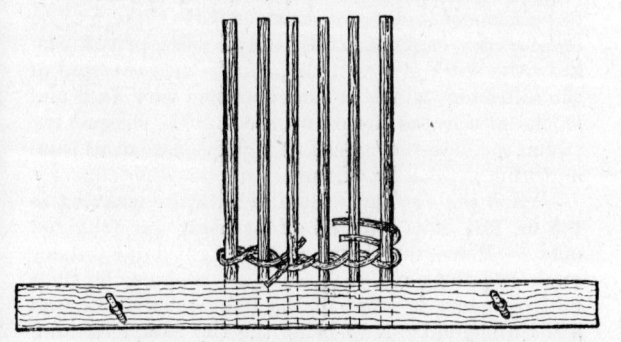

Fig. 33.—Basket Bottom in Screw-block.

the thumb press against the outside ones. This must be done to obtain a good-shaped bottom.

The side towards the worker will be called the inside, so that all tops and butts of rods must be begun and finished at the outside—of course, with the exception of one butt at starting, also one at the finish, which will come inside.

The bottom is now filled in by simple weaving, one rod at a time. Always start a rod with its butt behind an odd number; it is much easier to bring the rod round the outside sticks towards the worker than in the reverse direction. Suppose the tops of the two rods which were commenced with end behind the third stick on the right-hand side; place the butt of the first weaving rod behind the same stick, in front of the second stick, behind and round the outside stick, and so work the rod up; do not put the next rod on the same stick, but distribute the butt ends behind each of the four inside sticks. As the work proceeds, frequently apply the measure for width, as, unless the width is regular, the basket will not be well shaped. The work is tapped down close by using the iron (Fig. 8, p. 12) between the sticks. The thickness of this iron ($\frac{3}{8}$ in.) allows it to be used between any sticks or stakes likely to be employed. It is not much used on a low-priced basket; the work is closed sufficiently with the side of the left hand, which in time becomes very hard and thick, so that, as the osiers are quickly slipped between the stakes or sticks, it is used instead of iron, and thus saves a lot of time.

When the bottom is filled in with the weaving to $16\frac{1}{2}$ in. full, it is finished off by using one long rod only. Place this between the right-hand outside stick and the next stick, so that the butt, or thick end, projects in front of the five other sticks and a little beyond. Now bring the top round the outside stick, behind the fifth stick, leave it in front of the fourth stick, work the butt over behind the fourth and in front of the third stick, again the top over the butt, behind the third, and leave it in front of the second; lastly, the butt behind the second, and left against the outside stick. Cut the two ends neatly, so that they cannot slip from the position in which they were left (see Fig. 34). This will be sufficient to prevent the weaving coming undone, as quickness has to be considered in every part of basket making.

Now with the iron tap the work to the length (17 in.), unscrew the block, and take the bottom out. With the picking knife carefully cut off all the butts and tops in a slanting fashion, so that they may rest against the sticks and not be able to slip through.

When the bottom is neatly picked, cut off all the ends of the sticks and it is ready for staking.

Next, the bottom will require stakes driven in on all sides to receive the randing (weaving), with which the sides are to be filled in. These stakes will require to be about half the thickness of the sticks, and just long enough to finish in the border of the basket. All the stakes will have to be pointed at the ends with the shop knife (Fig. 4, p. 11).

The end of each stake is given two slanting cuts

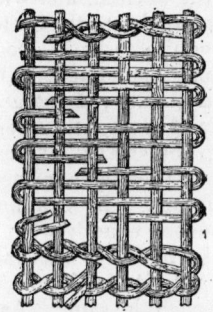

Fig. 34.—Simple Weaving.

about 2½ in. long, one down the back, and one at the side; these form a nice point for driving into the bottom. Seventeen pairs of these stakes will be required, ten for each side and seven for each end. These square baskets look much neater and more finished if they have corner sticks, so that, as the randing is worked tightly round, it leaves a nice bold corner.

In staking the bottom, first rest one end of the work-board on the sitting-board, insert something under the other end to make the board level, wet just the cut ends of the stakes, lay the bottom on the levelled board, so that one end is flush with one of the sides of the board, kneel on the bottom, and commence pushing the stakes down beside each stick. The third stick from the right will require one stake pushed in each side of it. The way to put them in is to clasp them tightly with the left hand just above the cut part; use the right hand as a mallet up and down the stake; each downward blow on the left hand forces the stake in. Just up to the commencement of the cut part will be far enough to drive them.

Now take the picking knife in the right hand and force the point gently into the stake to about its centre, close to the bottom, and with the left hand bend it up at right angles to the bottom. Of course, the stakes will require to be in good working order for this operation. None ought to be broken if the osiers are of good quality; if one gets broken, draw it out with a pair of pincers, and replace it.

In bending up the stakes, give the knife a slight twist so as to open the stake at one side, but leave the under side intact. By examining any staked basket, it will be seen exactly what is meant.

After the stake has been satisfactorily bent up, let it drop back again to its former position, and so proceed, serving each the same. As the basket is to have corner sticks, pick out the thinnest stakes to drive in nearest each corner, and the thickest in the middle of the ends and sides. When both ends have been staked, the sides are placed flush with the edge of the board, and holes will first have to be made with the large bodkin. Hold this in the left hand, and by means of the iron drive it through the centre of the stick at about $\frac{1}{2}$ in. from the end in such a way that the point of the bodkin comes up inside the basket. Always drive the bodkin with the flat part of the iron; do not use the edge, or the wood handle will be split. To make the driving as easy as possible, fill a hollow bone or an old end of cow-horn with a halfpenny tallow candle; do not remove the wick, as it holds the grease together. If the bodkin point is pushed into the grease-horn before it is driven into the stick, it can be twisted out again; if not, it can be removed by giving it several side taps with the iron. The moment the bodkin is removed, drive in a wet pointed stake, exactly as was done in the ends. Now drive another in at $\frac{1}{2}$ in. from the other end of the side. Next find the middle distance between these two, and mark it with a pencil if desired. At $\frac{3}{4}$ in. each side of this mark drive in a stake, so that there will be $1\frac{1}{2}$ in.

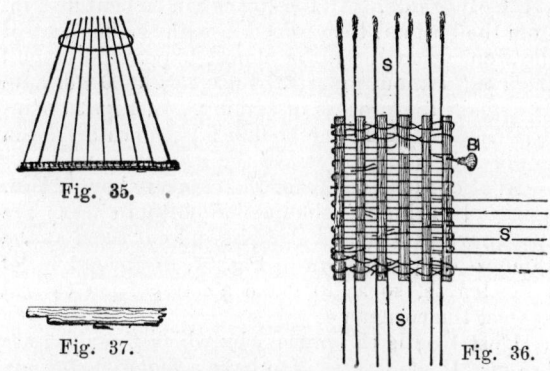

Fig. 35.

Fig. 37.

Fig. 36.

Fig 35.—Hooping Stakes; Fig. 36.—Staking Basket Bottom; Fig. 37.—Corner Stick.

clear space between them. Again find the middle of the space between the end and one of the middle stakes, drive one there, one at each side of the same stake, and space them so that they may be about two fingers' width ($1\frac{1}{2}$ in. more or less) apart; serve the remaining space the same. The ten stakes then will be in that side of the bottom.

If the worker has only a small workshop or room, it will be best now to gather the stakes up one at a time with the right hand and support them with the left arm bent round to receive them. Now take a small wood hoop not quite as large as the bottom—one can be made with a stout osier. Its use is

c

simply to support the stakes until fair progress has been made with the sides of the basket. Place the tops of the stakes in this hoop (see Fig. 35), when the left arm will be free; twist one of the tops round the hoop to prevent it working off—say the fifth one in the side from the left-hand corner. The remaining side has now to be staked, and the tops to be placed in the hoop with the others. Of course, the hoop will have to be tied with the fifth stake top as at the other side. All the stakes can be bent up $\frac{1}{2}$ in. from the bottom, then forced in with the flat part of the iron, when it will be almost impossible to pull them out without pincers. Figs. 35 and 36 will help to explain the process of staking. In Fig. 36 s indicates the stakes; the bodkin B is shown driven in to open the stick to receive the stakes.

Next cut four sticks for the corners about $12\frac{1}{2}$ in. long and as thick as the outside bottom sticks; see that they are nice and straight and cut them at the thinnest end, as shown in Fig. 37, to about 1 in. of their length, so as to make a flat portion to rest against the corners.

Upsetting is the process by which the sides are begun. If the basket is to have a foot rim, the upsetting is done by working three osier rods alternately, otherwise four rods are used. First see that all the stakes are fairly straight and in position. Then take three osiers, the same length and thickness, so that the tops may commence at the left-hand corner of either side of the bottom and finish at about the middle of the other side. Now place the staked bottom on the work-board, with a weight of some kind resting on it; for the weight an old flat-iron will do, but small lumps of lead, with a hole through the centre, are best, as they can be pegged to the bottom with a small bodkin, which will prevent them shifting about. The worker should now seat himself on the sitting-board, with his box seat placed behind him, and commence upsetting at the

GROCERS' SQUARE BASKETS.

left-hand end of either side. The first three upset rods are shown at A, B, C, Fig. 38. Place the top A behind the first stake, close in the bend; the stake must be pulled a little to make the rods lie in close and tight. Place B behind the second stake, and C behind the third stake. Now pick up A again, pass it over B and C in front of the second and third stakes, behind the fourth, and leave it in front of the fifth stake. Now pass B over C and A behind the

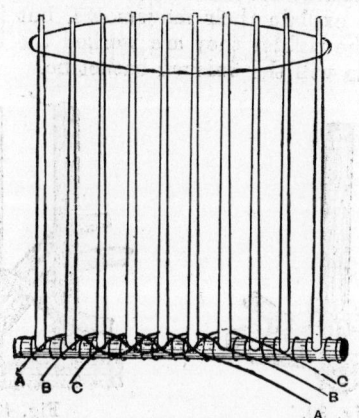

Fig. 38.—Upsetting Sides of Basket.

fifth stake, leaving it in front of the sixth, and so continue, picking up the last rod and passing it forward over the other two, behind the next unoccupied stake, and bringing in front, ready to be worked again in its turn. It should be noticed that all tops of rods are begun and finished outside the basket, whereas the butts are all commenced inside, except where they are pieced; in that case one will lie inside and the other outside.

When the corners are reached one of the four sticks will have to be put in. To do this, pick up the osier rod that was last moved, bring it forward as usual, and bend it round tightly against the corner; place the stick with the flat cut part upon it; keep it there with the left hand, and, with the right hand, bring the next rod to move tightly over the outside of the stick; hold it there whilst bringing the remaining rod tightly over the last, on the stick, as shown in Fig. 39, and behind the first stake in the end. The letter references in Fig. 39 agree with Fig. 38.

The illustrations show all rods worked very loosely to explain their movements, but in actual working the tighter they are worked the better in all respects will the finished basket be.

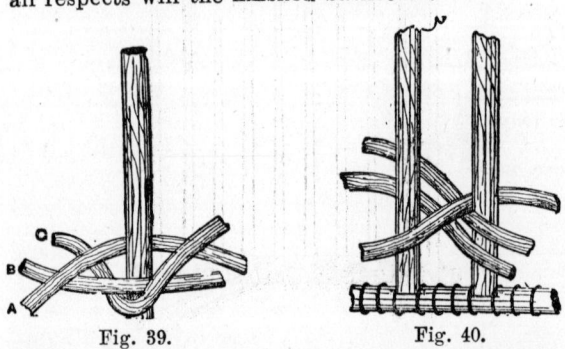

Fig. 39.   Fig. 40.

Fig. 39.—Fixing Corner Stick; Fig. 40.—Piecing in Upsetting.

Next, the other upset rod on the corner stick is worked behind the second end stake; then the one behind the corner stick, against which the 1 in. flat cut part rests, is carried forward behind the third stake. Continue in this way exactly as in the side until the next corner is reached, where the same operation is to be repeated as at the first corner.

When the butt ends are worked as far as they will go, leave each in front of a stake, projecting an inch or so as the case may be. Then take three more rods the same thickness and piece each one in its turn. This is done by placing a butt end beside the finished end, so that one butt projects outside and the other inside (see Fig. 40). Thus the upsetting is continued with these three fresh rods; the other two corner sticks are worked in, and their top ends are finished at the right-hand end of the side on which we commenced upsetting. To make the upsetting look about equal, another row now is put on; but this time commence the top ends at the left end of the opposite side. It will then be seen that having the butt ends on each side gives a good foundation for the sides of the basket. This second round is done exactly like the first, except that it is commenced, pieced, and finished at opposite sides to the first round. It will be best to cut off the six outside butts of the upsetting neat and close, as otherwise they would catch and prevent the basket going round freely.

The sides are filled in by simple weaving, or randing as it is termed. Take about three or four double handfuls of small osier rods; these will be of different lengths, perhaps from 15 in. to 3 ft. or more; but, by arranging them in their different lengths, they will exactly suit the purpose. Lay the longest rods at the right-hand side of the sitting-board, and those of the next length on the first lot, but at right angles. Continue in this way, keeping each length separate, until the longest and thickest rods are at the bottom and the short and thin ones on the top, ready to begin work with them. Place the rods in such a position that their butt ends are easily reached with the right hand when working.

The easiest and most pleasant part of the work—weaving the drawn osier rods one at a time in and out of the stakes—has now to be done. The practised workman does this very quickly. Sit on the board, the work resting on the work-board, and the latter resting on the legs or on a small block of wood, and begin at the first stake at the left hand of either side. Place the butt end of the first weaving rod just behind the stake. Now place it between the first and second fingers of the right hand. Of course, it must lie there loosely, so that the two fingers may slide along; it must not be removed from between the fingers, except where absolutely necessary. The thumb and the end of the first finger jerk it behind a stake, where it is immediately drawn into the crotch by the second finger, passed in front of the next stake, again jerked behind the next, and so on until the rod is worked up, remembering to leave its thin end projecting outside. As the rod is worked in and out of the stakes the work will have to be turned, when the corners are reached, towards the right hand. The work-board should be tolerably smooth, as the work has to be continually swung round, backwards and forwards. When the rod has been worked up, swing the work back to the starting place, and put the butt of the second rod behind the second stake, work it up, leaving the end in front of the next stake, beyond where the first rod finished (see Fig. 41). In this figure c c show the corner sticks, H handle space, and s stakes.

In this way the weaving in of the rods is continued, beginning with the butt end, one stake forward each time, until the basket is about 10 in. deep. Take about two stakes each side of the corner sticks out of the hoop. If the middle ones are removed, which should not be done until the sides are about 5 in. or 6 in. deep, strainers must be put across. Strainers simply are small rods, shaped as shown in Fig. 42, p. 41, and pushed down beside a stake in the weaving. The beginner had better have two of these strainers—one across each end of the side of the basket, say down beside the third stake from each end of the basket. The ends do not often require strainers, but, if they do, put one in the middle from end to end. Of course, the hoop cramps the worker a trifle, and the sooner it can be removed the better;

GROCERS' SQUARE BASKETS.

but if it is taken off too soon it is impossible to keep the stakes in an upright position.

For the bow handle across the top, space must be left between the two middle stakes in each of the sides the entire depth of the weaving. As each weaving rod reaches this point it is passed in front

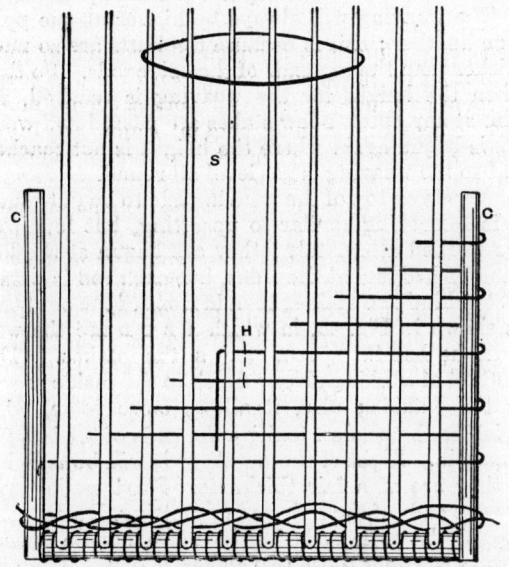

Fig. 41.—Weaving Sides of Basket.

or at the back, as the case may be, of these two stakes as though they were one stake. Thus there will be a 1½ in. clear space to receive the stick that forms the bow for the handle.

When a corner stick is reached, cut a point to the weaving rod, and push it down near the left-hand side of the stick; bend it down and work it up; doing this as each corner stick is reached helps to keep them firm.

Try to keep the measurements true; if, for example, the corner sticks at the sides were 18½ in. apart (outside measurement) at the start, do not let them be more than 19 in. apart at the top; the ½-in. spring will be an improvement rather than otherwise. The same remark applies to the ends; a basket drawn in at the top has a bad appearance.

The weaving will always be higher at one point than another; this is because the butts are so much thicker than the top ends of the osier rods. So that, when the height for the weaving is reached, say 9 in. at any point, a few stakes are passed and weaving is begun again where the height is not reached, and so the weaving is got level all round.

A wale on top of the weaving has to be put round. It is something similar to upsetting, but four rods are worked alternately; they are begun at the left-hand end of one of the sides, but each rod is passed first behind two stakes, then in front of the next two, as shown in Fig. 43, in which A B C D are the wale rods, H handle space, and S the stakes. This method of working gives a finish to the inside as well as the outside; also, it allows more room, when finishing the border, to drive the ends of the last few stakes in. Eight of these wale rods will be sufficient if they are of a fair thickness. Start waling with the top ends of the rods, as in upsetting. Do not work any of the wale rods between the handle space; always consider those two stakes as one. When the corners are reached, pick up No. 4 from the corner stick, and pass it behind the last stake and between the corner stick and the first stake in the end of the basket. Next pick up No. 3; place it behind the corner stick and out between the first and second stake in the end. Next No. 2 is to be held on the corner stick, and, whilst it is held there, No. 1 must be brought over it and behind the first and second stakes in the end, and left in front, of course. Now No. 2 is placed behind the second and third stakes and brought out to the front. The work is straightforward now until the next corner is reached, which requires exactly the same treatment as the first. Piece the butts of the wale rods, as the upsetting was done; also finish the tops of the last four rods at the right-hand corner of the side at which waling was begun. Fig. 44, p. 44, illustrates the method of waling the corners, B and C corresponding to B and C in Fig. 43.

Now see that the work to the top of the waling is level at all points by standing the stick measure beside the basket; if it is not, tap it down at any

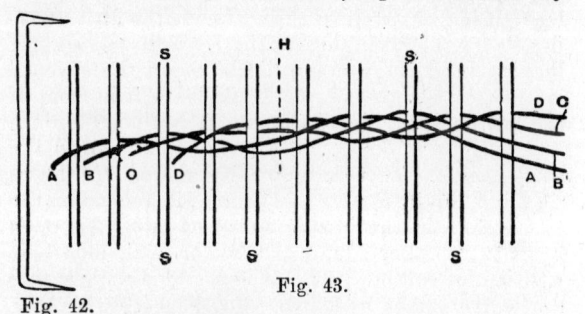

Fig. 42.

Fig. 43.

Fig. 42.—Strainer; Fig. 43.—Waling.

point with the edge of the iron. Then with the shears cut off what remains of the corner sticks quite level with the top of the waling.

Bordering is now begun. First cut four stakes the same thickness as those in the basket above the wale. Make a hole in the top of each corner stick with the large bodkin, and drive them in. If the stakes are at all dry, wet each one well by running the sponge along from the wale to the tip ends, then lay the basket on its side for a short time; an old, damp piece of cloth thrown over the stakes greatly helps in making them pliable. Begin at the third stake at the left-hand end of one of the sides.

This and the next three or four stakes are bent at right angles with the point of the picking knife, at about ½ in. from the wale. As each stake is bent down, let its top lie towards the right-hand corner stick; let it spring back to its upright position, and serve the other three or four in the same way. The left-hand stake in the handle space is not to be bent or used at all, but left in a standing position. Go back to the third stake (the first one bent), and with the left hand pass it behind the fourth, fifth, and sixth, leaving it in front of the seventh. Now pass the fourth behind the fifth, sixth, and seventh, and leave it in front of the eighth. Leave the fifth standing, bend the sixth behind the seventh and eighth, leaving it in front of the ninth; bend the seventh behind the eighth and ninth, and leave it in front of the tenth; lastly, bend the eighth behind the ninth and tenth, and leave it in front of the stake in the corner stick. There are now five stakes laid down, each behind the next two in front of it, reckoning the two stakes in the handle space as one. All open baskets, whether square, round, or oval, look best with a nice full border; this is got by always laying down five stakes as above. For baskets with lids, only four are laid down to start with; the lid having to cover the border, the dimensions of the latter have to be kept down as much as possible. Taking up the top of the first stake laid down, the third from the corner, pass it over the four other tops, also in front of stakes Nos. 7, 8, 9, and 10, and behind the corner stake. Now with the left hand grasp the ninth stake tightly and give it a sharp twist, at the same time bending it down and placing it behind the corner stake beside the top of the third stake. Now serve the tenth stake in the same way, placing it in between the ninth and the third stake tops. These three tops must lie quite level beside each other; this is repeated at each corner only. Care must be taken to keep these from springing back by letting the right arm project over them. Hold the fourth stake in front of the corner stake while picking up the fifth and laying it beside the fourth quite level; now bend the sixth stake over the fourth and fifth, and behind the first stake in the end of the basket, and out in front of the second. Now the seventh is to be crossed over in front of the sixth as close and tight as possible, and carried behind the second in the end and in front of the third. Next the corner stake must be bent down, and placed behind the second—of course, lying beside the seventh; always leave the tops out in front. Next bend the fifth over the fourth and behind the third in the end; bend down the first stake in the end and place it beside the fifth, leaving it in front of the fourth standing stake. Now pick up the fourth or the last at the corner, and pass it behind the fourth stake in the end; again bend down the second stake, and place it beside the last one moved.

The bordering may seem rather puzzling, but it is really very simple, with the exception of the corners. It amounts to this—the last projecting top to the left is carried forward in front of four stakes, and placed behind the fifth or unoccupied stake. Now the last standing stake (to the left) is bent down, and laid beside this top. These two actions are repeated with a slight difference at the corners, and Figs. 45 and 46 will, it is hoped, make the method of working corners quite plain. In both of these figures, H denotes the handle space.

As each stake is bent down and passed behind the two in front of it and out in front, to be again passed in front of No. 4 and behind the fifth and out in front of the sixth, it is finished, not being worked again, but being, with any others, cut off close with the picking knife when the corners have been worked to. The last upright stake, bent down beside it, takes its place when its turn comes to be moved. This is shown at F (Fig. 46).

44   BASKET WORK.

The full border at the corner (Fig. 46) has been begun; this is continued, the other three corners being worked exactly the same. On arriving at the last two stakes standing, the point where the border was begun will have been reached. The first from the corner is bent down, passed behind the second,

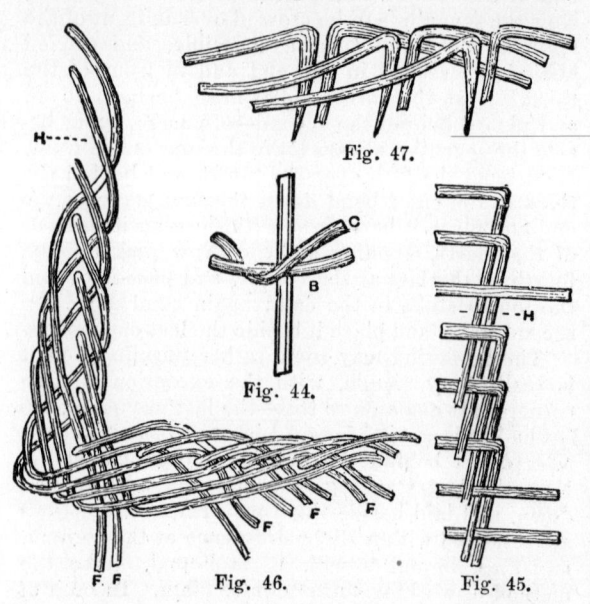

Fig 44.—Waling round Corner Sticks; Fig. 45.—Side View of Bordering; Fig. 46.—Top View of Bordering; Fig. 47.—Cramming.

and its top end pushed in the ½ in. space between the third and fourth, pulled tightly through, and left in front of the fourth. The second is then bent down and pulled through the ½-in. space between the fourth and fifth stakes, and left in front of the fifth. The stakes have now all been bent down to form the border. The full border is now made up to the right-hand corner by the process known as "cramming." As each top is brought forward, in front of four stakes, it is bent at right angles, pointed with the shop knife, and tapped down beside the fifth stake (see Fig. 47). In the basket under consideration the cramming will finish at the last stake in the side. Pull every stake as tight as possible; the work looks neater and better for it. If any stake tops have been left projecting, cut them off neat and close.

The basket can now be picked—that is, every butt and top of the weaving must be cut, so that each rests against the stake at which it began and finished. The picking knife must be in good order; one good way to sharpen it is to rub it on an emery-stick, made by tacking emery-cloth or emery-paper to a stick of wood; draw the knives sharply along first one side, then the other. It will be seen from the shape of the picking knife (Fg. 3, p. 11) that its purpose is to give a thrusting or pushing cut. Be very careful not to cut the weaving under the butts; use just sufficient force to cut the butt clean off. Commence inside the top, and work round to the bottom. To pick the outside, the worker should place the basket between his legs with the top ends pointing towards him; cut them all slanting a little, and let them rest against the stake at which they finished. The outside of the basket must be perfectly smooth, so that when in use the tops may not catch in the user's clothes.

Before putting in the bow stick (Fig. 48) for the handle, the foot rim must be put on. To do this, turn the basket bottom upwards on the work-board, and cut some stakes about the size of the largest that were used in weaving; some of the thickest of the stake tops that were cut off will come in for this. Cut these stakes on the bow or bellied side and push them down at the left-hand side of each stake, and one in each corner stick; of course, holes must be made in the corner sticks with the bodkin the same as in bordering.

When all the rim stakes are put in, upset them exactly as the basket was done, but only once round —that is, only six upset rods are used. Begin upsetting at the left-hand end of one of the sides; piece the three butts in the middle of the opposite side, and finish the tops of those used for piecing at the right-hand corner of the side at which the upsetting was begun. With the iron, tap down the upsetting, and commence to lay down the stakes as in the border. When four stakes have been laid down, go back to the first one laid down, pass it in front of three stakes, and behind the fourth or unoccupied stake and out in front; that stake is then finished. Now lay down the last standing stake to the left beside the finished one and out in front, ready to be passed in front of three in its turn. These two actions are repeated all round with slight difference at the corners. This bordering is spoken of as inside two and outside three. Every stake is in turn so used. Fig. 49 illustrates the bordering of the foot rim. A and B show the last two standing stakes being pulled under the two first laid down. C and D show the beginning of the cramming, and F shows the finish of the stakes.

A thick stick, well soaked, is bent to a bow shape to form the handle, which will have to be covered by working over it four long, rather thick osiers. First cut the butt end of the stick on the bow side similar to the stakes, dip it in the pail of water, and push it down one of the handle spaces so that its point stops against the upsetting. Now carefully bend it over so that it may form a nice-shaped bow, as Fig. 48. Some prefer high handles and others low; the lower they are, of course, the stronger they are. About 8 in. or 9 in. above the border at the highest part of the bow is a fair height. When the stick has been bent over to the opposite space, hold

GROCERS' SQUARE BASKETS. 47

it down, outside the basket, and stand the yard stick on the centre of the bottom to measure the required height, which will be about 20 in. to the highest part of the under side of the bow. Then cut the stick to about the right length, letting the cuts of both ends of the bow be towards the inside of the basket. After both ends are in the handle spaces, the iron

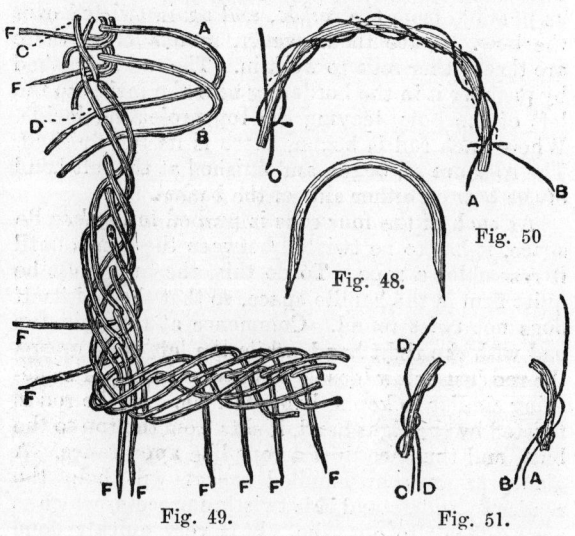

Fig. 48.

Fig. 49.

Fig. 50.

Fig. 51.

Fig. 48.—Bow for Basket-Handle; Fig. 49.—Bordering Foot Rim; Figs. 50 and 51.—Lapping Handle Bow.

can be used to force either side down if too high, or it can be pulled up if too low. To make the handle somewhat shouldered, put the knee firmly on the highest part and carefully pull up with one hand on either side to form the shoulders, at the same time pressing the centre down with the knee.

The next operation will be to cover the bow completely with twisted rods from the top of one handle space to the other. For this are required four long smooth osier rods, pointed at their ends, and of sufficient length to be pushed down the handle space and twisted round the bow four or five times, according to their thickness. Then a hole is made with the bodkin between the wale and the weaving at the left side of the bow from the outside; the top of the twisted rod is pushed through, pulled up as tightly as possible from the inside, and again twisted over the bow. Space them evenly, remembering there are three other rods to work in. The rod is finished by pushing it in the bordering near the inside to the left of the bow, leaving the top projecting inside. Where each rod is begun, there is its top finished. The rods are all begun and finished at the left hand of the bow on either side of the basket.

As each of the four rods is pushed in the handle space, it has to be twisted between the hands until it resembles a rope. To do this, the butt must be quite firm in the handle space, so that the rod itself does not twist round. Commence at the thin top end with the right hand, while the left hand grasps the rod just below loosely to prevent kinks, or something similar to knots, being formed. As the rod is twisted by the right hand, it slits from the top to the butt, and thus acquires a rope-like appearance. A glance at any bow-handled basket will help the reader to understand this twisting process, which is very difficult to describe. It is very quickly done with a little practice; in fact, the bow ought to be lapped with the four rods in five minutes easily. In Fig. 50, A shows the beginning of the first rod, C that of the second, and B the finished top of the rod to be pushed into the border. The beginning of the third rod is shown at B (Fig. 51), and of the fourth rod at D. Let each rod lie in its proper groove, in close contact with the bow, and twist the rope-like rods closer together as they are wrapped round the bow. Pull every rod as tight as possible. Cut off the four ends of the handle rods inside the basket.

CHAPTER IV.

ROUND BASKETS.

ROUND baskets, known also as cobs, are begun by what is termed "laying a slarth" under the feet of the workman (see Fig. 52). For the round cob under consideration, cut four sticks about 11 in. long; shave each along the middle with the knife on the bow sides so that one pair may cross the other, the four cuts being uppermost when placed under the feet. Take two small rods and cut a point at the butt end of one; the butt of the other will have to form a half stick in the slarth, as four and a half sticks are required to form the bottom. On the board between the operator's feet two of the sticks should be laid close together, cuts upward; the second two should be laid across them, and held firmly in position by placing a foot on each of the ends. Take the uncut rod I (Fig. 52), place it over and then under A and B, and lay it level with C and D. Then bend the same rod over C D, then under E and F very tightly, at the same time pulling E and F upwards a little; pass over G and H and under A and B again. At the cut portion of A B, push in the point of the second tie-rod J; bend up A B a little whilst bringing the first rod up between A B and C D. Let it lie there by tightly passing the second rod over it, under the half stick, and C D; carry it round over E F, under G H, over A B.

Now work the two tops alternately round to A B, which must be opened by bringing between them the top at the back, and then passing between them the other top to the back. Continue thus opening all the sticks, working up the two rods; there will then

D

be nine separate parts to receive the weaving (see Figs. 53 and 54). Always endeavour to have a crown to the bottoms, whether these are oval or round; it prevents them giving way when anything heavy is

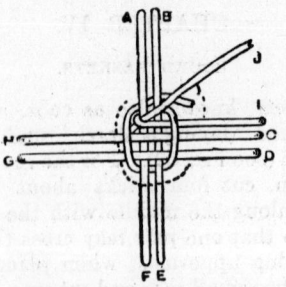

Fig. 52.—Round Slarth.

put in the finished basket; this can only be successfully done when tying the slarth. Next fill in by working two rods together; this process is known by basket makers as "slewing." Keep the forepart

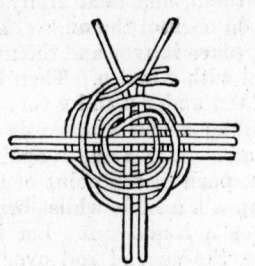

Fig. 53.—Working Tie-rods together.

of the left foot on the bottom, place a butt in front of a stick, then behind the one to the right, and so continue adding a rod now and then until the bottom measures 7½ in. across; then pair off by pointing two rods, pushing each in the slewing at the left of two of the sticks, working them over each other and between the sticks until the bottom is 8 in. across. Push the ends in the pairing and pick the bottom, cutting the sticks off with the shears. In Fig. 54 A shows the finish of the tying rods; B, C, D, E are single rods to form the slew, and G H are the pairing or finishing-off rods. F shows how the rods are worked.

Now cut eight and a half pairs of stakes, as described for the grocer's square basket (p. 31), and

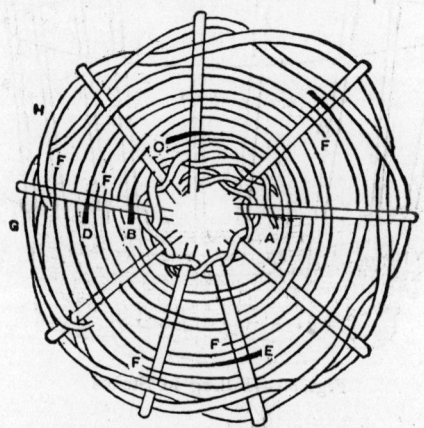

Fig. 54.—Bottom of Round Basket.

put them in the bottom, one down each side of eight of the sticks, the ninth stick receiving only one. Prick each up with the picking knife; afterwards gather them up and place in a hoop several times larger than the bottom, as these cobs require a spring of 3 in. at the borders. Drive in the stakes with the flat of the iron level with the ends of sticks, and upset the stakes. The neatest way is to begin with the top ends of upsetting rods; discard from 7 in. to 9 in. of tops by cutting them off the four rods; the starting will then be more substantial. Now push the top end of each of the rods in the weaving by the side of four of the stakes; proceed as in the case of the square basket (p. 35) round to the right—passing each rod in front of three stakes, behind the fourth unoccupied stake, and so on. Whenever the four rod upsetting reaches its starting-point, one butt or top, whichever it may be, is dropped, and only three rods are continued; each will then pass in front of

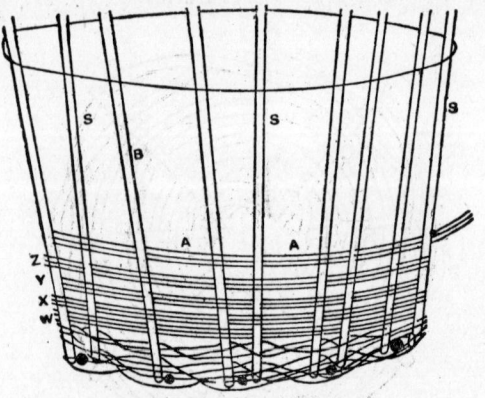

Fig. 55.—Filling in Stakes

two stakes, and behind, and out at the third stake. Piece the butts with three other rods, and work them up. Either run the small bodkin through the crown of the bottom between the sticks and force its point into the work-board, or use a weight on the bottom only, and begin filling in the stakes with slewing. Fig. 55 shows the filling in with a slew of three rods: A shows the slew, B an odd stake, S stakes in pairs at each of the eight sticks; W the full slew which goes completely round the basket, coming in front of the stake at X, going round again as at Y, in front of Z, and so on.

ROUND BASKETS.

From the upsetting there must be a gradual spring to the border, where the measurement must be 11 in. across at 11 in. deep. A round of white rods about halfway up helps to brighten the appearance of the basket. Start slewing with one rod, add another a few stakes farther on, add a third still farther, and continue this three-rod slew; as the tops get finished outside, keep adding a butt inside, continually working round to the right. To level off, work either a two-rod or one-rod slew, as may be necessary, and pair off with two rods, piecing their butts; the border then can be laid down. Perhaps

Fig. 56.—Border for Round Basket.

the beginner had better prepare a place to insert the handle bow. Point two thick pieces of stick and push down the slewing, beside a stake at opposite sides, so that the bow may cross exactly over the centre of the open top. Of course, these sticks will have to be drawn out again when the border is finished.

For the border, lay down five stakes, and proceed as in the square basket, except that there are no corners to trouble about. Fig. 56 shows the method of forming the border, A being the first stake laid down, and B B finished stakes. After finishing the border by cramming, squeeze the sponge upon the two pieces of sticks and pull them out. Point, bend, and push in the stick to form the bow handle, lap it exactly as for a square basket, and the cob will be finished.

For the better class of white randed cobs, the rods are drawn in their different lengths, and worked in the sides one at a time; also nine pairs of stakes can be used, as an odd one is not a necessity in randing as in slewing. The bottom is paired to its proper size by working two rods together, as shown by the tie-rods in Fig. 53.

CHAPTER V.

OVAL BASKETS.

As an example of oval basket work, a linen basket may be described. The bottom is begun under the workman's feet, as in round work, by tying a slarth. Eight rods are used in properly tying both small and large slarths, which differ only in length and thickness. The slarth is generally laid about half the length of the finished bottom, that is, from opposite points of the two tie-rods first bent round. In bottoms up to 14 in., three lays of bottom sticks are used; for larger sizes four trays are required, also thicker sticks. For a 14 in. bottom, cut seven sticks about 12 in. long; shave a little off along their middle as for the round cob sticks (see p. 49); also cut a piece of rod 8 in. long to divide the eight tie-rods. This 8-in. piece is required only in the three-lay slarth.

Lay the sticks and the eight tie-rods on the board within reach; take four of the rods and place the butt ends under the right foot, quite level (see Fig. 57). At about 5 in. from the extreme ends pick up A and C; put two of the sticks in between these two and between B and D; drop A and C, and pick up B and D; place in between B and D and A and C three sticks about 2¾ in. from the first two; drop B and D, again picking up A and C, and placing in the last two sticks so that the three lays may be in a 7-in. space. Now take the 8 in. piece, and place it so that it may lie under the three middle sticks, its ends resting on top of the two outside lays of sticks, where they are finally cut off neatly, as shown at H (Fig. 57).

The other four rods are now worked, one at a

time, between the sticks E, F, G, their butts the opposite way to the first four, as shown at I J K L (Fig. 58). Tap the rods as close together as

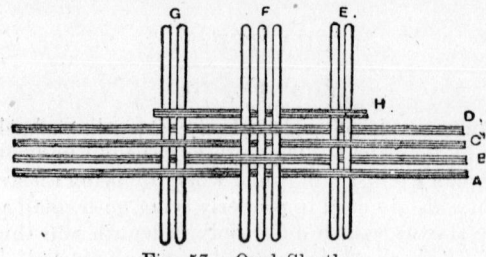

Fig. 57.—Oval Slarth.

possible by using the iron between the sticks. Keep the feet firmly on the right-hand end and side commenced at; pick up D, pass it very tightly over I J K L, then under the two sticks G, over F, under E;

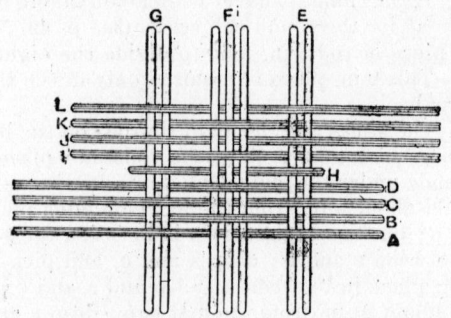

Fig. 58.—Slarth Rods in Position.

leave each projecting as shown. Now pull up I by the side of J, also K between J and L; whilst holding I and K pass C under I J K L, over G, under F, and over E. B and A are worked just like D and C. Do not forget to pull up the sticks a little every time a rod

OVAL BASKETS. 57

passes under them; the object of this is to give a crown to the bottom (see Fig. 59). All the tie-rods will now be projecting at one end of the slarth; turn it round and hammer A B C D close. Then work I J K L round that end, exactly as the opposite end was done. By pulling the four butts to the left whilst working round them they are got in line as nearly as possible. Before opening the sticks, D C

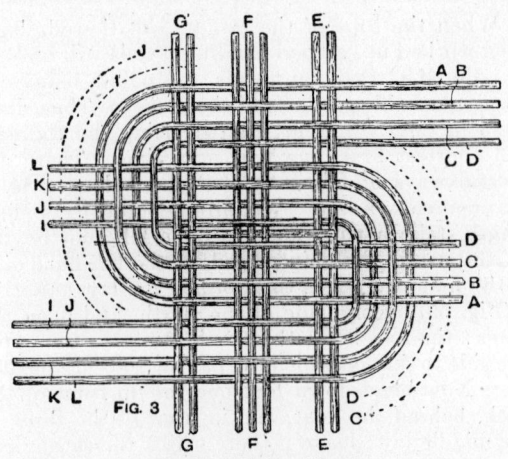

Fig. 59.—Tying Slarth.

and I J must be worked in the same manner as the first two at each end. After that the tops of the tie-rods are worked round in pairs, and in between those sticks that require to be opened. Perhaps the end sticks will be the best to commence at. These four, say A B C D, must be divided into three separate portions to receive the pairing and finally the stakes; pull D to the left, work in A and B between D and C, push A to the right, again working the tops of A and B between the butts A and B; the butts C and B are not divided at either end. Open the sticks E, leaving sticks F undivided. Now serve I J K L exactly the same way; with L K open G, then open E with I and J, then work round to the other tops, when C and D will have to be worked again by opening the sticks G on that side of the slarth. Now the required number of sticks is opened; the tops are simply paired under and over each other between the sticks, and are so finished up.

When the tops of the last pair of tie-rods have been worked up, a good handful of rods will have to be pointed at their butt ends, the points being cut the reverse side to those of the stakes. Then draw them in their different lengths, using the thinnest and shortest first, one pair at a time. There are several ways of filling up, but the following is as neat and close as any: Wet all the points of the first length, take a pair, and with the left foot on the slarth push in the pointed rods at the left-hand side of the first two sticks that formed the lays—that is, E (Fig. 59) on one side of the slarth, and G on the other; the foot holds the slarth firmly on the opposite side to that on which the pairing rods are pushed in. Now bend down first one rod in front of the stick, behind the next, and in front of the three of the middle lay; leave it there whilst the second rod is served the same, and so work them up under and over each other. Start the next pair at the left side of F and E or G (whichever it may be), and so continue at either side until the bottom is 14 in. lengthways. When a slarth is laid half the length of the finished bottom the workman does not trouble to measure for width; it will be proportionate in all sizes. By laying the slarth shorter or longer there is easily obtained a bottom wider or narrower for special purposes. Finish off the bottom by pushing the ends of the last pair in and out of the pairing, pick off the ends neatly, and with the shears cut off the ends of the sticks whilst they are held under

OVAL BASKETS.

the foot. Fig. 60 illustrates the method of opening the bottom sticks, the letter references agreeing with those on Fig. 59.

Stakes for the bottom can now be cut the same as for the round basket described on p. 51. Sixteen pairs are required for a randed basket; for a slewed basket manage to have an odd one, say fifteen and a half pairs, putting the odd one where two of the sticks happen to be closer together. Wet the points of the stakes, stand with one foot on the bottom, and push in the stakes—a pair to each stick—at either side of the stick. Of course, the three middle sticks

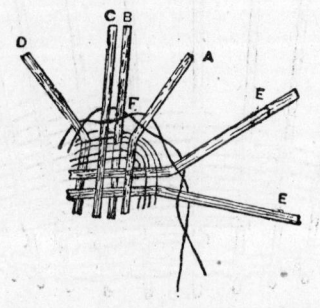

Fig. 60.—Opening Bottom Sticks.

in each of the sides and the pair at each end are reckoned only as single sticks. After all the stakes are in, turn all completely over, and gently force the bottom down on the board; put the right foot lightly on the bottom, and prick up each stake in turn; afterwards place them in a large hoop. Now sit on the board and drive in the stakes closely by using the iron on their bends.

Begin upsetting with the top ends of four rods at the left-hand shoulder of either side (as the bottom lies before the worker) by pushing in the cut top ends at the side of four stakes. Work the rods in front of three stakes and behind and out of the fourth or unoccupied stake. If the rods are short, they will have to be left unfinished at the curve on the other side of the bottom, while four more rods are pushed in exactly as at the first side and worked round to the first tops, when one is dropped and three are worked on the first four, outside two stakes and inside one. If the first four rods are sufficiently long to go right round the bottom and lap over their own tops, that will be found most convenient. The

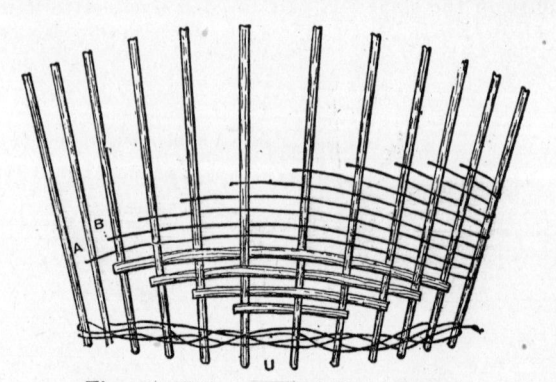

Fig. 61.—Siding up Oval Linen Basket.

butts of the two sets, or the one set, whichever is used, must be pieced with three other rods at the sides and worked up. Another round of upsetting can be worked on top of this, if preferred; it is always advisable to have a good foundation of upsetting on any basket. Cut off any butts protruding, and then prepare the randing by drawing some small rods into their different lengths. Pull the stakes at both ends of the bottom out of the hoop, only leaving in a few at either side, as these baskets require a good spring of 8 in. at the top from end to end. Weave in a few short pieces at both sides first to

raise the latter a trifle; work these in as shown in
Fig. 61, in which figure it will be noticed that the
butts as well as the tops are left projecting outside
the basket, as the inside requires to be as smooth
as possible. After working four or five short pieces at
both sides, commence the randing by placing the first
rod as shown at A (Fig. 61), and work it up; swing
the work back and place in B, and so on, working
round to the right until the proper height is reached

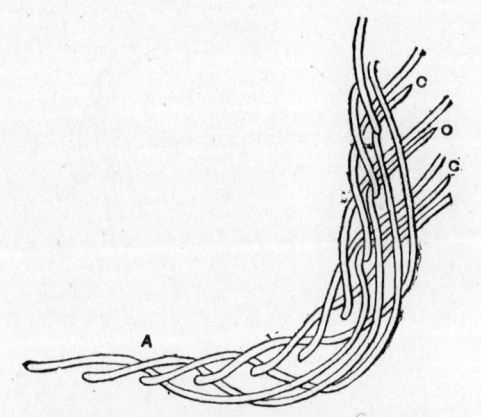

Fig. 62.—Bordering Oval Linen Basket.

—namely, 7 in. at the ends, when the measurement
should be 22 in. across from end to end. Raise the
sides about 2½ in. higher than the ends by working
a few rods along each side until they are of equal
depth, when a wale of three or four rods, as preferred, can be worked round, commencing at one
side and piecing the butts at the opposite side, working them up. If three wale rods are used, work each
alternately inside two stakes and outside one; if
four are used, inside two and outside two is the
method, and, of course, this gives a better finish both

inside and outside the basket. The four wale rods that are pieced with are worked right up, overlapping the tops of the commencing four.

The border is commenced at the left hand (A, Fig. 62) by laying down five rods, and working each in front of four stakes and behind two, as described in connection with the grocer's square basket in Chapter III. and the round basket in Chapter IV. The first three stakes finished are seen at C. When

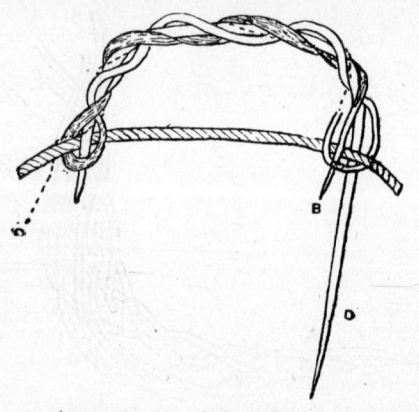

Fig. 63.—Handle of Oval Linen Basket.

the border has been finished by cramming, the butts and tops can be carefully trimmed off with the picking knife, holding the basket sideways between the knees.

Two handles are put on, one at each end; for these, cut four rods, press in the basket with one foot, and push in two of the rods from the top of the border beside a stake and about three or four stakes apart, or wide enough to allow of the hand passing between them. Bend the left-hand rod A (Fig. 63), and pass its top under the border from the outside at the right-hand side of the second rod B, and pull it inside the basket, just leaving sufficient outside to form a bow, on which the other rod and its own top are lapped. Twist the second rod rope fashion, lap it over the bow three times, push its end in under the border (outside), pull it through, again lapping it over the bow three times, and then under the border at the right-hand side; pull it through, lap it over

Fig. 64.—Turning back Rod in making Handle.

for the third time, and leave it outside the border hanging down. Next twist the bow rod top first pulled through, and lap it round the bow by the side of the second rod; it is worked three times across the bow (three laps each time, of course), and then it is pushed in between the two rods and its own butt, where they go through the border (outside); both the tops are pulled tightly down and cut off close. Fig. 63 explains the method of working the handle, and Fig. 64 shows how the rod D (Fig. 63) is turned back at the second turn across the bow.

CHAPTER VI.

FLAT FRUIT BASKETS.

BASKET workers make up numbers of flat fruit baskets in slack time, and quickly dispose of them at the beginning of a promising fruit season. Any rough, brown osiers can be worked in the bottoms of these flat baskets, but the osiers must be made pliable by soaking in water, as fully described on p. 12.

The flat basket under consideration is commonly known as a 3-peck, which appears to be the size in favour.

First cut eight sticks (brown, of course, are cheapest) about 17 in. long; pick out the two thickest for the outside ones, and put them in the screw-block, 19½ in. apart outside measure; put the others in as described for the grocer's square basket (see Fig. 33, p. 29). Begin and finish the bottom in the same way, working the roughest of the osiers in the weaving. After the bottom is finished, take it out of the block and carefully trim it with the picking knife. If a quantity of these flat baskets is required, it is much the best to make one or two dozen bottoms straight away; then what is left of the weaving can be tied up, so as to make a clearance for sorting and cutting stakes. The sides will require nine stakes driven in the weaving beside the sticks, and seven in the ends, driven through the sticks after making holes with the bodkin. Put in the eight thickest stakes at the corners.

After all the stakes are in and pricked up, put them in a hoop and commence upsetting. Eight white osiers are generally used first, as they relieve

FLAT FRUIT BASKETS.

the dark-brown colour of the basket. Point the eight rods with the shop knife, and make an opening with the bodkin at the left of the first stake at the left-hand end of either of the 19½ in. sides of the bottom. Drive a pointed upset rod in there, one in the weaving beside the first stake in the side, one in to the left of the second stake, and a fourth to the left of the third stake. As the flats have no foot rim, this method of beginning is preferable, as the butts take the wear better. To upset with four

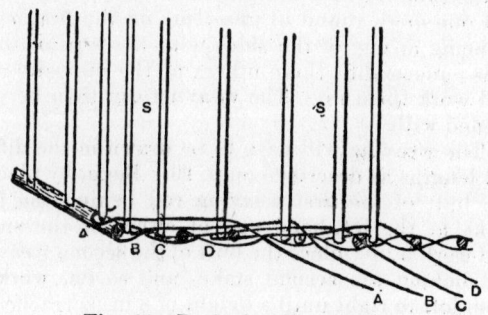

Fig. 65.—Beginning Flat Basket.

rods, the workman must sit higher, with the edge of the work between his knees, as the upsetting has to be pulled as closely as possible in the bend of each stake so that the edge of the weaving may be covered. Now bend the first upset rod tightly round the corner in front of the two corner stakes; also in front of the second in the side; place it behind the third close in the bend, and leave it in front of the fourth The second rod is then bent, placed behind the fourth, and out in front. Continue in this way, taking up the last to the left, passing it in front of three stakes, behind the fourth unoccupied stake, and out in front of the fifth, ready to be passed on in its turn (see Fig. 65, where A B C D are the upset

E

rods, and s the stakes). When the left-hand corner of the opposite side is reached, put in the other four upset rods exactly as were the first; the tops of the first four must be left at the end until the second four have been worked along the side, when the first tops can be proceeded with. The top that first reaches the first upset rod finishes there, while the three others are worked round the corner and along the side, in front of two stakes, and behind the third alternately. Finish the second lot of tops in the same way; place the work on the board, and put one more round of upsetting on the first, commencing at one of the sides with the tops of three rods; piece with three others at the opposite side and work them up. The weaving can then be proceeded with.

The weaving will have to be drawn in the different lengths as described on p. 29. Begin by placing the butt of the first weaving rod behind the first stake at the left-hand end of either of the sides, and work it up; place the butt of the second weaving rod behind the second stake, and so on, working from left to right until a height of 8 in. is reached at all points, outside measure.

Two handles now will have to be made, one on each end. One rather stiff rod is used for each; push its pointed butt down the weaving, beside and at the right-hand of the third stake from the right-hand side. Twist the rod from the top downwards, to give it a rope-like appearance; now push its top through the weaving at about $1\frac{1}{2}$ in. from the top of same to the left of the fifth stake, and draw it through from the inside, leaving sufficient outside to form a bow. Bring the top over the weaving to the right of the same stake, twist it over the bow three times, push it through the weaving to the right of the third stake, and bring over the weaving to the left of the third stake. Now twist it in its proper groove along the bow, push it between the

FLAT FRUIT BASKETS.

rod in front of the fifth stake, work it back again, and finish it in the weaving at the third stake (see Fig. 66, where B shows the beginning and F the finish). Another way to form the handle, as used on white flats and on all good hampers, is to use two rods, pushing one down to the right of the third stake, the other to the left of the fifth stake. Bend the one to the right down, and push it through the weaving to the left of the fifth stake and the pointed butt of the second handle-rod; pull it through the weaving, leaving sufficient outside to form a bow. Next twist the second rod rope-fashion, lap it over the bow of the first three times, then pass it

Fig. 66.—Handle of Flat Basket.

through the weaving, over the latter, back again to the fifth stake, back again for the third time, and finish its top in the weaving at the third stake. The top of the first rod, which was left lying across the basket inside, is now twisted and lapped over the bow three times through the weaving—over, back again the second time, its top being pushed between the open space in front of the fifth stake; it is then worked back for the third time, and finished where the first did. It should be understood that each time a handle-rod is pushed in the weaving at one side of a stake it crosses the stake at the back and comes forward again at the other side of the same stake; the reason for this is obvious. After the handles are finished, if one side of the basket happens to look neater than the other, let that be the front of the flat.

Now, with two rods, beginning with their tops at the left of the side intended to be the back of the basket, proceed to pair off, as it is called. Place the first top behind the second stake, its extreme tip end resting outside the first stake, the long part projecting in front of the third stake. Place the

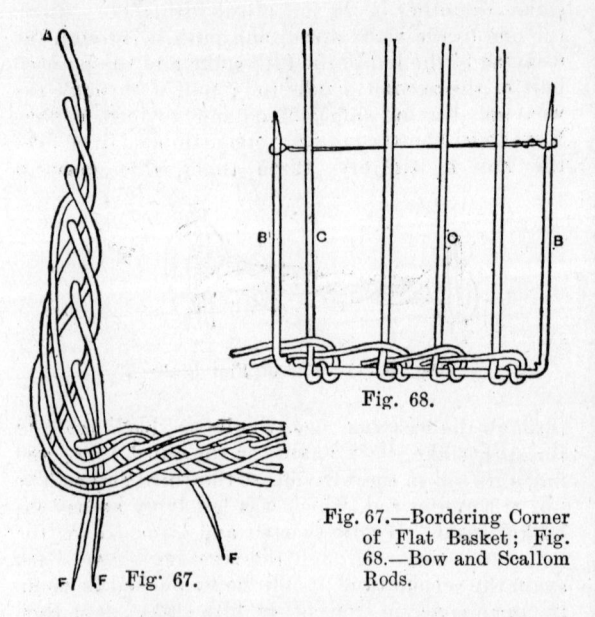

Fig. 67.—Bordering Corner of Flat Basket; Fig. 68.—Bow and Scallom Rods.

second rod behind the third, its tip end in front of the second stake, with its long part in front of the fourth; now work the two rods alternately over each other, behind a stake each time, and out in front. Piece the butts at the front side, and work the tops of the piece rods round, finishing on the tops of the first two.

The border is made by laying down the third, fourth, fifth, and sixth stakes at the side where pairing was begun. Next pass the third in front of three stakes and behind the last in the side; lay down the seventh and eighth at the side of the third, bring the fourth in front of the seventh, eighth, and ninth, and behind the first in the end; lay the last in the side, beside the fourth. Place the fifth in front of the last two in the side, also the first in the end and behind the second, then the sixth in front of the last in the side, first and second in the end,

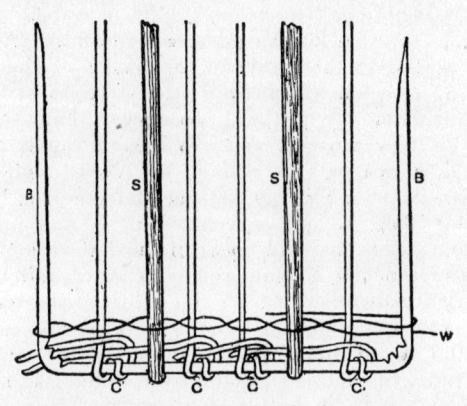

Fig. 69.—Beginning Basket Lid.

and behind the third lay the first stake in the end, beside the sixth, and so proceed at each corner. Fig. 67 will make this clear; in this, A is the first stake laid down, and F shows the finished stakes. After finishing the border by cramming, trim the basket inside and out, when a bow can be turned to form the lid.

The bow can be formed with one long stick, or in two parts by two short ones; the latter method will, perhaps, be the best for a beginner. Place the flat so that the side that is to be the front will be to the right hand. Lay the butt of a stick along the front border; at the right-hand corner nearest the worker cut three notches, to help in bending it to the shape of the corner (keep the bow near the outside edge of border); cut three other notches at the left-hand corner, and then bend the bow to the shape of the basket. Tie a strainer across, keeping the bow just the width of the flat, measuring from the outside edges of the border. Next cut two thick sticks a little longer than the length of the flat outside; extra thick ones split in halves are the most suitable for the purpose; the flat part is to be placed to the inside of the basket. Almost any kind of wood will answer; the strength of the lid depends mostly on these two sticks. Four scallom rods now are cut, and are lapped round the bow, as shown in Figs. 68 and 69. Next bind in the two sticks (s, Fig. 69), resting their ends on the bow B. Take a long weaving rod w, and push sufficient of its butt end between the left corner of bow and the first scallom rod c to lap round the bow-stick and project across the width of the bow. Bend it closely round the bow, behind the first scallom, and out in front. Now take one of the sticks (sometimes the end is shaved a trifle wedge-shaped, which makes it lie better until woven firmly in), place it on the bow and the top of the rod, pass the butt tightly over it, and behind the two scallom rods. Place the top in front of the second scallom and behind the third; move the butt in front of the third, place the second stick on the butt, and work the top over the stick, behind the fourth scallom. Lastly, place the butt in front of the fourth and behind the bow-stick; cut it off there, bend the top round the bow, and work it in and out the scalloms and sticks (Fig. 69). This particular make of lid seems to be used on fruit flats exclusively. After weaving a few inches the workman sits astride it, on the body of the flat turned bottom upwards.

FLAT FRUIT BASKETS.

Begin most of the weaving rods behind the two thick sticks, and every two or three tops work round the sticks from one to the other (only just the thin ends); this helps to completely cover up the sticks. When 5 in. have been worked, a space must be left at each side for tying on the lid, as shown at A (Figs. 70 and 71). Instead of weaving round the bow, turn the rods round each of the outside scallops about three times. Next point a butt, push it down the weaving beside the bow, in front of the lid, lap it round the bow-stick three or four times, and work it

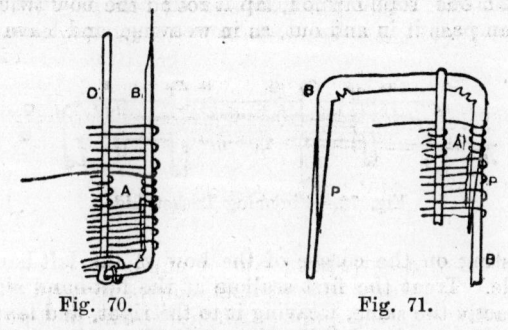

Fig. 70.   Fig. 71.

Fig. 70.—Front of Basket Lid; Fig. 71.—Piecing Bow.

up. In Fig. 70, B is the bow, and C one of the scallops. The left side must not be lapped. Point the ends of the bow, letting the cuts face each other. The worker should sit on the lid, in order to work more quickly. To guard against drawing the bow inwards, occasionally measure it on the body of the flat. When the weaving has reached to within a few inches of the next two tying spaces, the other part of the bow must be bent and notched to complete the lid. The cut points of this part must be made on each outside, so that, when it is pushed in the weaving, each cut will face the cuts of the first part of the bow. At about 15½ in. make similar tying-on spaces to the first. But, before lapping the pointed rod round the bow, push the thickest part of the second bow in the weaving beside the thickest end of the first; then push the thin end down beside that of the first; do not forget to wet the ends. To make the bow, cover the border exactly; it will have to be placed on the flat and gently tapped down with the iron (see Fig. 71). Now lap the front tying space and fill in the bow with weaving. Well wet the four scallom-rod tops A, B, C, D (Fig. 72), and work them as follows: Twist the first right-hand one rope-fashion, lap it round the bow twice, then pass it in and out, as in weaving, and leave it

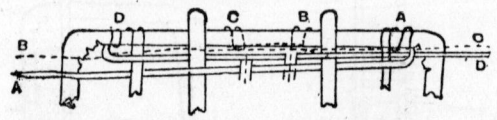

Fig. 72.—Finishing Basket Lid.

resting on the corner of the bow at the left-hand side. Treat the first scallom at the left-hand side exactly the same, weaving it to the right, and leave its top on the right-hand corner of the bow; pull each very tightly. Next twist the right-hand one of the two middle ones, working it to the left; lastly, the left-hand one, working it to the right; cut off the four tops, neatly resting on the bow at either side. The iron must be used rather freely on these lids to force the weaving rods close together, and especially the last few inches, as the worker cannot use his hand there, on account of the bow end being in the way. Pick the lid neatly; it can then be tied on the side of the border that was crammed. Fig. 73 illustrates the method of doing this. Cut a point at the butt end of two smooth rods; place the lid in position on the border of the flat; with the bodkin make a way down the weaving beside a stake from the top of the border directly under a space in the lid; push down the point of the tie-rod G and twist it rope-fashion; pass it over the 1 in. of bare bow; push the bodkin in the space, slanting under the border, and out at the outside of the basket

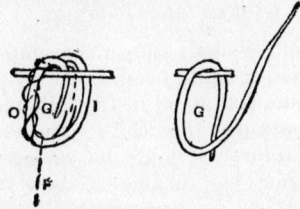

Fig. 73.—Tying-on Basket Lid.

marked o in Fig. 73. Push in the tip end of the tie-rod, and pull it up through the space at the outside of the lid; now pass it to the right of the butt, lap it over the bow formed twice, pass it again under the border up through the space, and again twist it over, letting the twists lie even, as in the handles; cut the top off at the left side, where it was pushed through in the first place.

CHAPTER VII.

WICKER ELBOW-CHAIRS.

THE wicker elbow-chair shown complete by Fig. 74 is one that has actually been made on the basis of the instructions contained in the following chapter. Before attempting the chair, the contents of previous chapters should be mastered. The chair is begun by turning a bow—that is, a long, thick stick is bent with the hands and the help of the workman's knee to the shape shown at B (Fig. 75, p. 76). The width of the bow when bent to shape is 18 in. full, and its length must be sufficient to receive 20 in. of weaving. Tie the bow across with an osier or a piece of string A near where the weaving will finish; use as much of the thick end of the stick as possible in forming the bow. Eight scallom rods (s, Fig. 75) must now be cut; these will have to be very long, as they are lapped round the bow, receive the weaving, form the front of foot of chair, and finish in the foot border. Each of the butt ends is cut, as shown in Fig. 76, to about $5\frac{1}{2}$ in. Now commence lapping them round the bow as made clear in Fig. 75. Begin at the right-hand side; place the commencement of the cut part over the bow, underneath, then pull up tight, and pass it over the scallom rod itself; then each end is bound in the lap of the succeeding scalloms, as shown.

With two small rods begin filling in as illustrated by Fig. 33, p. 29. Then fill up with simple weaving. When about 3 in. has been worked, place the work in the screw-block indicated by dotted lines (Fig. 77), and screw up tight. The left-hand side of the bow will require another stick placed beside it to strengthen it. Cut a stick about 20 in. long, point the thin end, and push it in the weaving, beside this thin side of the bow. Next cut two stakes and push them in (one at each side) between the scalloms and bow, and open them with the weaving as shown at

Fig. 74.—Wicker Elbow-chair.

B B (Fig. 77, p. 77). The thickened portion at A represents a stick pushed into the weaving to strengthen one side of the bow.

For a distance of 20 in. (the distance ought to have been pencilled before screwing in the block) continue weaving in and out the ten rods round the bow, removing the strainer after 5 in. or 6 in. has been weaved, so as to work quickly.

The iron (Fig. 8, p. 12) must be used frequently to drive the weaving close together. When 19½ in. has been worked, use two small rods with which to finish off; this time place about 9 in. of butt behind the two sticks of the bow. Bring the butt round the bow, behind the first upright rod, and leave it in front of the third. Now pick up the top part of the same rod, place it over the butt, behind the third, and

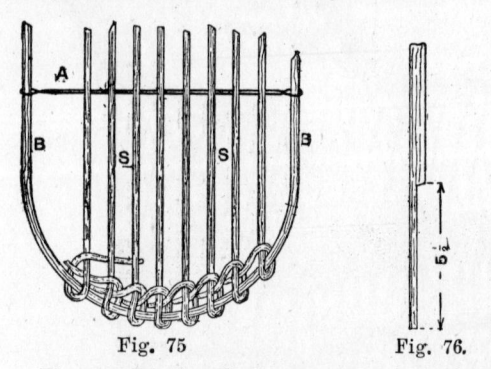

Fig. 75   Fig. 76.

Fig. 75.—Lapping Scalloms on Bow; Fig. 76.—Cut Butt End.

leave it in front of the fourth. Piece the butt with another rod by pushing in butt by butt, and so work them over each other, in and out the uprights. After turning them round the thick part of the bow, work them neatly into the weaving, back again to about the fourth upright, and cut both tops off at the back.

Take the seat out of the block, being careful not to break any portion of the projecting scalloms; pick the longest rough ends of the weaving, not too close, so that the ends cannot slip through when the chair has been much used. Cut off the ends of the bow with the shears, or with a tenon saw if the butt

WICKER ELBOW-CHAIRS.

is very thick; also, if the scallomns are well soaked, kneel on the rough side of the seat, and, with the picking-knife point, open them and bend them up at right angles, exactly as described on p. 32.

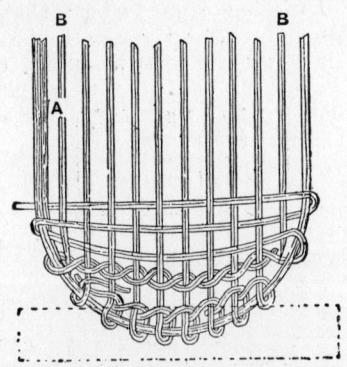

Fig. 77.—Weaving Chair Seat.

The seat will now require to have stakes driven in all round the bow to form the foot of the chair. The chair being described has rather a deeper foot than most, being 14 in. from the seat bottom to the

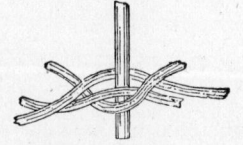

Fig. 78.—Working Sticks in Upsetting.

border that it stands upon. This is a comfortable height, but chairs are made as low as 6 in. or 7 in.; it is a matter of choice. The extra depth will involve a little more work and rather longer stakes. Two thick, straight sticks will be required, 25 in. long, quite free from knots, as after the foot of the chair is finished these sticks have to be driven through the work with the iron to form the arms of the chair. These sticks are worked in the upsetting (shown on an enlarged scale by Fig. 78) on each end of the bow stick; take a slight shaving off each thin end. Cut sixteen pairs of stakes, and push one in down the weaving beside each bow,

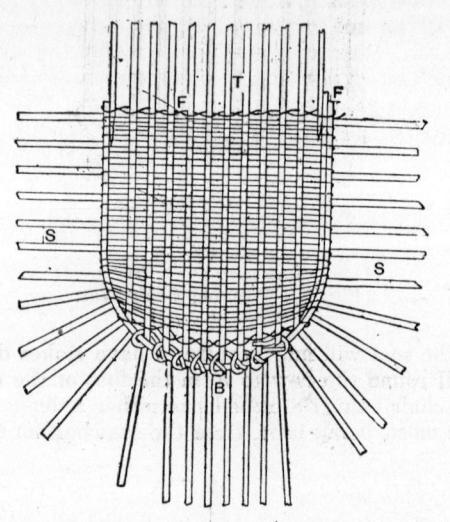

Fig. 79.—Staking Chair Seat.

prick, and bend them up, and let each drop back again. Pick out eight of the thickest stakes, and, after driving the bodkin through the bow and down beside each of the scalloms, quickly push in a wet-pointed stake; prick and bend these eight. Next drive in eleven in each side of the bow. When they have all been opened with a knife-point, force in with the iron, place them in a hoop nearly the size of the seat, and tie the hoop with a stake top in front and back to prevent it working off. For the method of staking, see Fig. 79, where B shows the back of the chair, F the front, S the stakes, and T the scalloms, now forming stakes.

Upsetting (see Fig. 80) is the next process, working three rods alternately, always working round to the right; begin at the left-hand side, as the seat rests on the board, with the tops of rods, and work exactly as shown by Figs. 38, 39, and 40 (see pp. 35 and 36). Work in the two sticks at the extreme corners (see Fig. 78), and piece the butts of the upsetting at the right-hand side, and let these finish

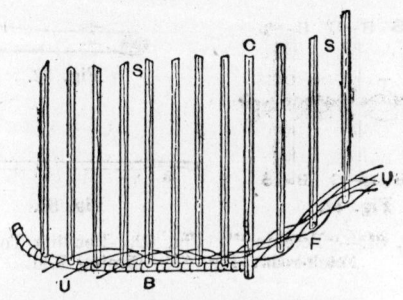

Fig. 80.—Upsetting Foot of Chair.

at the left side for the first complete round. The tops of the second round begin at the right-hand side; they are pieced on the opposite side and worked up, forming the second round. The third round begins in front—that is, where weaving finished—at the left hand; it is pieced at the back and finished in front at the right hand. The fourth and last round begins at the back, is pieced in the front, and finished at the back by pushing each top end into the upsetting already done, and pulling tightly through to the front or outside. In Fig. 80, B is the bow representing the seat, F the front, S the stakes, U upsetting rods, and C the corner post.

As regards the open work, every stake except the ones at each side of the two front posts (or sticks) will require by-staking—that is, another stake is driven into the upsetting at the left-hand side of each of the first stakes. Rods that are not less than 16 in. will do for by-stakes, except about the second and third at the right-hand side of the two posts, which had better be of full length; of course, all the by-stakes, B, must correspond in thickness with the first stakes, S (see Fig. 81).

As the foot of this chair is several inches deeper than most chairs, it will need an intermediate

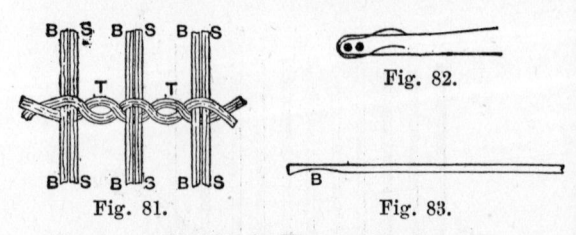

Fig. 81.—"Fetching"; Fig. 82.—Bending Tops of Fetch-rods; Fig. 83.—Piecing Rod.

"fetch," as the next proceeding is termed, for strength. A foot of 11 in., and under, will only require one fetch, just before waling and bordering off. The fetching is begun at the back, with the tops of two rods, by passing the top of one rod round a pair of the stakes at the right hand, the other top passing round from the left, thus binding the two stakes in the two rods and their tops by giving a twist of one rod and top together over its fellows. Often two twists will be required before binding in the next pair of stakes, especially at the curved parts, in order to give the foot a little "spring." But a little judgment will be necessary as to when one or two will be best. The process of fetching is shown on an enlarged scale by Fig. 81, in which figure S shows the stakes and B the by-stakes; T shows the twisting of the rods when this is needed for the spring of the foot, or to regulate the stakes. Fig. 82 shows how to bend the tops of the fetch-rods round the first pair of stakes. After every one or two twists of the rods (as the case may be) bind in the next two stakes very tightly between the two fetch-rods; take in the single stakes, those next the posts, just the same as if they were pairs. Be very careful not to draw the posts inwards, but keep them perfectly upright if three twists must be given to the fetch-rods, before binding the posts in them. Proceed along the front to the middle, where

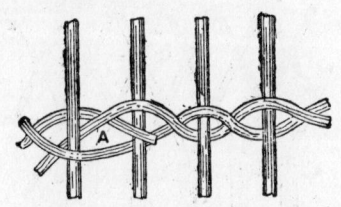

Fig. 84.—Piecing Fetching.

the two fetch-rods will require to be pieced with two others; see that they are long enough to go round the right side, and lap well over the first two at the back. The butts of the two piece-rods must be cut as shown at B (Fig. 83) to ensure a neat joint. When either of the first butts finishes, the cut butt of a piecing-rod is pushed in between them, binding the finished butt against the next two stakes, where it projects in front, to be eventually cut off, as shown at A (Fig. 84). Take two more rather stout rods, and begin their tops at the left-hand side, so that their butts will finish at the right-hand side. Place each top behind a pair of the stakes; now pick up, first one, then the other rod, placing each behind a pair of stakes, working them tightly.

F

The piece-rods for these will not require cutting, but need only be pushed in, as in upsetting; finish the tops by pushing in between the first. This first fetch should be about 6 in. from the seat.

Proceed with the second fetch before waling and bordering the foot-rim. Mark with a pencil at every few stakes a depth of 12 in. from the seat, resting the end of the measure on the board. Take two fetch-rods, as Fig. 82, and begin at the back;

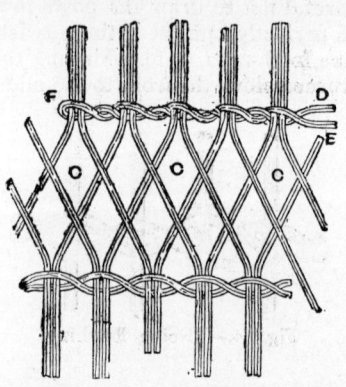

Fig. 85.—Fetches in Foot of Chair.

the rods are worked the same as the last, but the stakes must be crossed as shown in Fig. 85. The stakes are crossed, first passing a right-hand one from the bottom, C, behind two left-hand ones, and binding it with the third left-hand by-stake with the fetch-rods D and E; and so the fetching continues, first pulling a right-hand one (of a pair) to the right, then a left-hand one to meet it, and binding both tightly with the fetch-rods; every stake will cross two others. Fig. 85 will make this plain; F shows the commencement at the back of the foot. A little judgment must be used as to when it is advisable to give one or two twists to keep the pairs of stakes regular. Just before the corner posts are reached, push a stake in the first fetch beside the posts, at each side of them; these are simply to make the corners look close and full; they are each crossed in their turn. The right-hand stakes of the first pair to the left of both posts, and the left-hand one of each pair to the right of them, are bound in beside the posts as the fetch is worked round them. The fetch is pieced in front of the foot, exactly as the first. The stakes in the front of this chair-foot cross over three others, but this is only for appearance. When the last pair of stakes have been crossed and bound in at the back, simply work the tops of the two fetch-rods in and out of those stakes

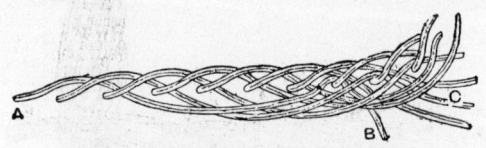

Fig. 86.—Bordering of Foot of Chair.

at the commencing point, and so work them up. Next on top of the fetch two rounds of waling will be required. This is worked exactly as in upsetting. Begin with the three tops at the left side of the front; piece the three butts at the back of the foot, and finish at the right side of the front. The next round commences at the back, is pieced in the front, and finished at the back. It will be noticed that all tops of waling, upsetting, and fetch-rods overlap somewhat; this helps to make up for the unequal size of butts and tops.

Before bordering the foot-rim, see that the points at the two curves, also at the two posts, are about 13 in. deep; if these points are a trifle deeper than any other part of the foot, the chair will stand quite firm when finished. Now, with the iron, tap down the waling at the centres of the sides, also at the back and front; that will make the points named a trifle high. Every by-stake of a pair that is right-handed will have to be carefully cut off with the shop-knife, leaving every original stake to be worked in the border.

The border is begun at the right side, about the third stake from the post (see A, Fig. 86). Lay this and the next four down, each behind the two in front of it, and left outside, until the five have been

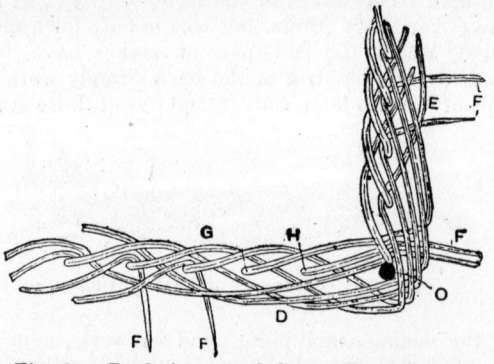

Fig. 87.—Bordering round Corner Post of Chair.

laid down. Then pick up the first one laid, pass it in front of four stakes and behind the fifth, which will be the finish of that stake, as shown at B. Lay down the first upright stake (that will be the sixth from the starting point) beside the finished stake, and so continue these two actions, leaving a finished top behind each stake, as shown in Fig. 86, until the posts are reached. C shows the finish of the second stake.

Work every rod as tightly as possible; the illustrations show very loose working to elucidate the method for the border. Fig. 87 shows how the border is worked round the posts; the only difference between this and the border of the grocer's square basket described on pp. 41 to 43 is that in each corner stick of the latter a stake is driven, but in the case of these chairs the posts must be quite free to allow them to be driven through the foot after it is finished.

The bordering is simply worked round them, as shown, and either of the stakes (or both) at the side is laid down in its turn. In Fig. 87, O indicates the post of the chair foot, D the left side, E the front, and F the finished stakes. At G and H the finishing tops are not shown, in order that the corners may be more clearly explained.

To finish the border, the last two standing stakes are drawn in between the first and second, and

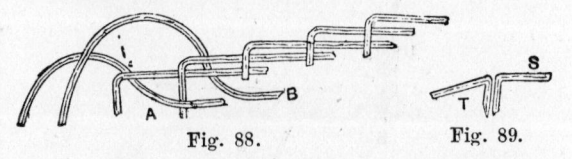

Fig. 88. Fig. 89.

Fig. 88.—Finishing Bordering; Fig. 89.—Cramming down Stakes.

second and third, of the laid down stakes, and pulled tightly, as shown in Fig. 88, which is a side view of the first laid stakes, A and B showing how the last two are worked under the first two.

The seven projecting tops are simply carried forward (each in its turn) in front of four stakes, gauged, and bent with the fingers and thumb, pointed, and crammed down beside the fifth stake, as shown in Fig. 89, where T is the top and S the stake. Do not forget to wet these points, and drive in with the iron.

Cut off each top of the finished stakes neatly and close in the border, and the ends of all butts and tops, inside and outside the foot. There are now the two posts projecting about 12 in. These must be well wetted, and driven through the foot until the thick ends are about level with the border. For convenience the feet of the chairs are worked upside down. Now that the posts have been driven through, the foot will stand in its proper position while the thin ends of the posts stand up above the seat ready to be utilised in the arms. See that the foot stands firm on its bordered rim; sometimes one or other of the posts will have to be driven back a trifle, so as to make the foot stand quite firm on any flat surface.

The back of the chair is begun by driving in stakes all round the foot in the upsetting, beside

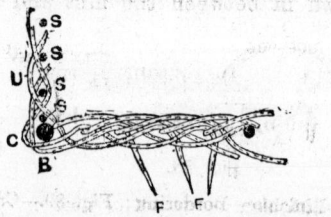

Fig. 90.—Bordering at Edge of Chair Seat.

each stake that was driven in the seat-bow. Those in the front are only small rods, those at the sides are about two sizes larger, whilst the back ones must be very long, as the back is to be 26 in. from the seat, and the tops of the stakes have to be worked to form the plaited border. Cut the points of all these stakes just the opposite side to those of the square basket described in Chapter III.; they are forced in with the two hands after the bodkin has been driven down where necessary, principally at the curves and the back; put all the points level and dip them in water, when they can be driven in easily. Drive the stakes down at the left-hand side of the foot stakes. If the points go right through the upsetting for $\frac{1}{2}$ in. or $\frac{3}{4}$ in., do not

WICKER ELBOW-CHAIRS.

trouble to cut them off until the chair is finished, when each can be cut off with the picking knife. When all the stakes have been driven in, one round of upsetting will be required; this begins at the left side. (In referring to the right and left side it must be understood that the workman is supposed to have the front of the chair before him.) Work the upsetting round the front, piece it at the opposite side with three smooth, long stakes, so that they may go beyond the left post, and push down a stake beside the post at the right hand. The front stakes will

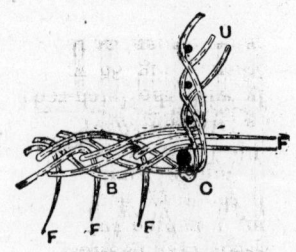

Fig. 91.—Finishing Bordering.

now have to form a border to give a finish to the chair and to keep the cushion in position. Proceed with the three upset rods round the post, as shown in Fig. 90; place U behind the post, leaving it in front of the first stake; now B is to be held in front of the post while C is crossed over B, placed behind the first stake, and left in front of the second. Now B is carried forward and placed behind the second clear stake and left in front of the third. Lay down the stake beside the post by the side of B when B is finished, and C takes its place in its turn. This border may be termed inside two and outside two, as each stake is laid down behind the two in front, then in its turn is placed in front of two and behind the third, and left finished in front of the fourth, and so on. Three of the stakes, when worked round the right-hand post, must be used as in upsetting again; see Fig. 91, where C is the right-hand post, F the finished tops, and U the continuation of the upsetting. If rather thin, piece them with three others and finish the latter by pushing their tops through the first upsetting and cutting them off outside. F, Fig. 90, shows finished tops.

All the stakes in the back and sides will now require by-staking with the exception of the first behind each post. They must correspond in thickness and length with the first stakes. They are pointed

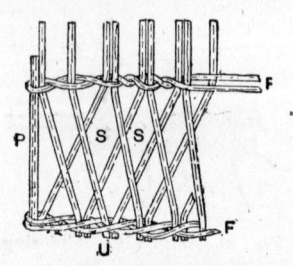

Fig. 92.—Beginning "Fetching."

in the same way, and pushed down the upsetting at the left side of the former stakes. After the pairing, stand the measure on the seat, and with a pencil mark a pair here and there, at about 7½ in. above the seat at the sides and 10 in. in middle of back, as a guide for the first fetch. The fetching is begun at the right-hand post (see Fig. 92). The two tops of the fetch-rods F are bent round the front of post P, at the same time binding in the first bystake, then giving the fetch-rods a twist over again and binding in between them the second by-stake. After this, bind in a pair each time to obtain the cross effect. The cross can be kept regular by giving either one or two twists to the fetch-rods before binding in each pair of stakes s. The fetching is now continued by passing the first stake forward behind the two by-stakes, then bringing the third by-stake to meet it, and binding in together; this action is continued round to the opposite post. When about 13½ in. is reached, the fetching must rise gradually round the curve, to be 10 in. above the seat at the back, where the butts of the fetching must be pieced, then sloping round the curve to correspond with the opposite one, and then straight at the pencil marks to form the arm. Before the post is reachd, push down a stake to the left of it, bind in with the post the first or right-

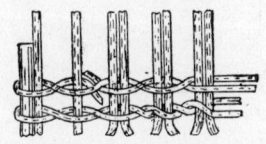

Fig. 93.—Working Pair of Rods on Fetch-rods.

hand stake of the last pair, bend the fetch-rod tops neatly round the post, one to the right and the other to the left, and work them back again, in and out along the arm; then cut off just the tips outside.

To give additional strength, it is advisable to work two other rods on top of the fetching. Begin at the post by placing one of the butts between the post and the first stake, then bring the butt tightly round the front of the post, work it behind the first stake, and leave it in front of the second. Pick up the long end, pass it over the butt behind the second, and leave it in front of the third. Piece the butt with the second rod, and so work up over and under each other, as shown in Fig. 93. As this back is deeper than most, another fetch must be put round, about 5 in. above the first, for strength; of course, the back may be made any height desired;

if it is 20 in. or 22 in. only two fetches will be required, leaving out the middle one. The second fetch is commenced at the third and fourth pair of stakes, behind the right-hand post, by placing the top of one of the fetch-rods in front of the third, passing behind the fourth, and leaving it in front of the fifth. Place the second top in front of the fourth pair, behind the fifth, and in front of the sixth. Continue as in the other fetching; let it rise gradually round the curve to the proper height, piece at back, slope at the second curve to correspond with the first, and finish the tops after the fashion of the beginning. Fig. 94 illustrates the beginning of the

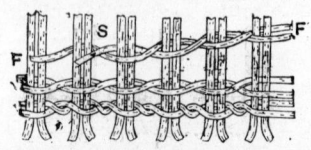

Fig. 94.—Beginning Second Fetch on Chair Back.

second fetch in the back of the chair, the starting and rise of the third fetch being clearly shown; s indicates the stakes; F F is the third pair of stakes from the post. The stakes need not be crossed in this fetch; it will be enough if they are simply paired. Work another pair of rods on top of the fetch-rods; begin the butts at the left side, in the same manner as the fetch-rods; work them tightly round the back, and finish their tops at the right-hand side. When working from the left to the right side, work inside the chair, kneeling on the seat. Any of the fetches can be tapped either up or down to make them look even, especially at the curves or shoulders. A little care and judgment are necessary to get the shoulders to correspond. A beginner should not hurry over them, as it looks odd to see in a finished chair the plait of one shoulder nearer to the front than the other.

The third and last fetch (H, Fig. 95) must now be put round the back; the stakes are crossed a little differently and fetched in singly. First mark the stakes at the back with the pencil to the desired height—in this chair 24 in.—to show where the fetch has to come; measure from the seat. Begin the fetch-rods as the first set, at the right-hand side; begin to open the stakes at the seventh pair. Fig. 95 will explain the crossing of this fetching better, perhaps, than any written explanation. The pair of stakes are opened thus: First A is bound in the fetch-rods, then C; next pass B forward

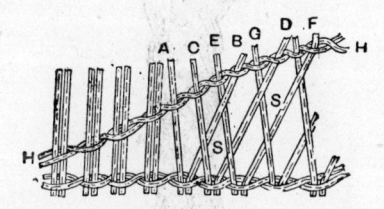

Fig. 95.—Crossing Stakes in "Fetching."

behind C and in front of E when E is fetched in; then fetch in B. Now pass D behind E, then in front of G when G is bound in, and so continue crossing the pairs round the back; let the slope of the shoulder correspond with the first. From shoulder to shoulder let the measurement be about 21 in. at the fetch-rods. To form a graceful curve for the shoulders, of course the fetching should be tightened or slackened, as may be required, or two twists may be necessary occasionally to regulate the stakes; also push down an extra stake at the side of the last pair to be opened at the right of them; open it, and bind it in the fetch in turn; it will help to give a closer plait. These fetch-rods are pieced at the back similarly to the first and second. The iron is used to obtain graceful curved shoulders and back to the chair before proceeding further. Next, from the left-hand post, work a pair of long rods on the fetch round the back as far as they will go. Place the butt of one rod between the left post and the first stakes, bring it round the post, pass it behind the first stakes, and leave it in front of the second pair. Pass the long part of the rod over the butt behind the second stakes, piece the butt, and work them up, kneeling on the seat. This process also is illustrated in Fig. 93, p. 89.

Fig. 96.—Plaiting Border.

Work, say, two pairs of rods round the back, beginning the butts of a pair at either side, on top of and at the rise of the fetching, as shown in Fig. 94, p. 90. See that the arms correspond in height, cut off the short ends of the posts, and finish with a plaited border. Carefully cut off the by-stakes in the arms, except when the original stake is thin, in which case the pair can be laid down as one stake. If the posts have been cut from a thin broomstick (this is excellent for the purpose), a hole must be bored with a gimlet down the centre for an inch or two, and a stake driven in; this is only required at

WICKER ELBOW-CHAIRS. 93

the right-hand post. If the post is a thin stick, then the by-stake behind it answers instead, and is not cut off with the others. Wet all the stakes thoroughly two or three times with the sponge, and place the chair on its side while cutting ten long, thin stakes to commence the plait. Drive these in the upsetting in front of the right-hand post, and commence plaiting them, standing at the side of the chair. First cross the pair A (Fig. 96) over the others, then B across A, next C over B, D over A and C, then E over B and D, and so continue as shown. When the plait has reached to the post top, each pair

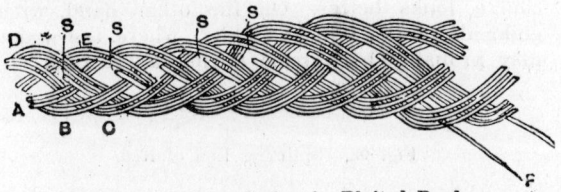

Fig. 97.—Bending Stakes in Plaited Border.

must be bent over in its turn, to continue along the arm; two pairs pass inside and three pairs outside. The plait in Fig. 97 will make this plain. First pass pair A over B and C in front of the first upright stake; leave them behind the second (in Fig. 97 the stakes are shown laid down). Bend D over E and A and beside the first stake, which is laid down with D as shown and held down; B is passed over C and D and between the second and third stakes, and left there; E is passed over A and B and laid beside the second stake, which is laid down with E. The three rods are held down whilst C is passed between the third and fourth stakes. When D is laid by the side of the first stake, and the latter is laid down, there are three working rods; the number must not exceed three, as when these are laid by the side of the sixth stake, and the latter is laid down, the working rods have increased to four. Simply leave the fourth (which will be the thinnest) in front of the next stake; that will be the finish of that rod (see F, Fig. 97). A top is to be finished at each stake as the work proceeds in exactly the same way. The stakes are lettered s.

At the top of the back the stakes will be nearer each other. If three working rods cause cramping, work two only by leaving a top (let it be the third from the workman) inside as well as the one left outside; or a stake may be cut off here and there, and then the three-rod plait continued, which, of course, looks better. On the other hand, when going down the other shoulder, where the stakes may probably be a trifle farther apart than any

Fig. 98.—Splitting End of Rod.

other part, and the tops of the back thinner, there is no objection to piece them here and there by pushing through a pointed rod from the inside to the right of the next three to move—of course, leaving the fourth, or thinnest, inside, to be cut off when the plaiting is finished. Always push the point under the plait, where it is not noticed in the least. When nearing the other post, drop one of the three working rods again and finish with two, to correspond with the first, and after laying down the last stake plait the five pairs so that the plait will, when bent down, over, and in front of the stick, reach a little below it. The plait is bent over the post, and it will then be found that sufficient has been plaited to cover the same.

Cut off clean and make neat all tops, either inside or out, just under the plait, so that they may not be noticed, also all butts in the piecing, and

WICKER ELBOW-CHAIRS.

then bind the beginning and the finish of the plait to the posts for a few inches with two skeins.

A brief description of how to produce the skeins from the osiers may be useful. If the worker does not possess the skein tools, he had better purchase a length of split cane and bind that round instead. First sort out, say, half a dozen smooth, long rods, then cut off a few inches of the tops, and with a knife (a pocket-knife answers well) just split the cut top end of the rod into three, as shown in Fig. 98;

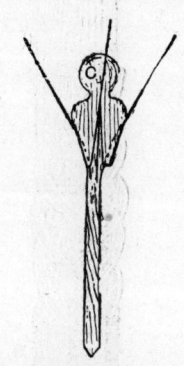

Fig. 99.—Inserting Cleave in Rod.

serve each rod the same. Now take the three-cleave illustrated by Fig. 12, p. 13, in the right hand, the opened top in the left, and insert it as shown in Fig. 99, so that each of the divided parts of the rod rests in a cut-out section of the cleave; push down the cleave, working the left hand down as well, but keeping the latter very near the cleave c; this is an important point. Some osiers will split readily, others will require soaking. After splitting them, dip or well wet them, take the shave (Fig. 16, p. 13), put a leather cot on the left thumb, sit a little above the board, lay the skeins handy at the feet, hold the shave in the left hand against the left knee, with the knife edge from the worker, and put in the top end of a skein, remembering it is the pith and heart of the rod that is to be removed, not any of the outside smooth part if it can be avoided. The shave must be regulated by the thumbscrew; the knife must be raised at first so as just to shave off a small portion of the pith. Press

Fig. 100.—Finishing off Chair Post.

on the skein with the covered thumb and draw the skein through towards the worker—one at a time, of course. When they have all passed through, lower the knife a trifle and take another shaving off from end to end. The osiers usually have to be run through three times, to leave just the required smooth outsides. A beginner had better run them through the shave four or five times rather than cut them in two. Shave them while wet, press well with the thumb, and keep the knee rather low. The right hand clasps the skein lower after each pull.

The chair now can be finished off. Cut the plait so that it may cover the front of the post, with just the ends touching the front border at the seat. Wet a couple of skeins, and push the wide end of one under the upsetting, as shown at U (Fig. 100); let it rest against the post P, pass the long part behind, and tightly bind the plaiting to the post as at S. Finish the skein by piercing through two of the plait rods, or near the outside of the post, with the awl. Push in the skein top, draw it tight, and cut it off, when the chair will be finished.

CHAPTER VIII.

BASKET BOTTLE-CASINGS.

Before casing stone bottles with wicker-work, it must be decided if the top part, from the neck to shoulder, shall be covered. Often a name and address are stamped on that part of the bottle, and then the casing begins at the bottom of the jar. If there is neither name nor handle, the top is covered first, from the neck to the shoulder. Some bottles are encased entirely with osiers, others have cane bottoms, and sometimes one or two cane handles. In this chapter the entire casing of a one-gallon bottle will be described.

First cut nine thin sticks a little longer than the distance from the neck to the shoulder. Take a long osier T B (Fig. 101) and bend it to make two working strands round the stick A, under the left foot; next bind, or "fetch" in, the eight other sticks S, as illustrated. When the ninth stick has been secured, take the whole from under the foot, and place the fetched ends closely round the neck of the jar, lap one of the strands completely round the neck to give a finish and hide the ends of the nine sticks; then, with the two working strands T B, bind in the first stick A (see Fig. 102), which will then lie next to the ninth stick T, Fig. 102. After the pairing in and out of three or four sticks, work a slew of two or three rods by adding rods D (see Fig. 103) until the edge of the shoulder is reached. In all slewed work the odd stake or stick is very convenient, as, by occasionally putting in a single weaving rod at a time, as the thin ends of the first are finished, it is possible to work continuously

BASKET BOTTLE-CASINGS.

round from the start to the finished depth of the basket (see Figs. 102 and 103). In Fig. 103 A shows the jar mouth, B the sticks, C the commencement of slew, and F the finished rod.

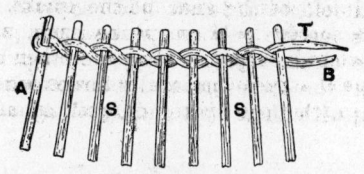

Fig. 101.—Beginning Cap of Bottle-casing.

It is advisable to work a single rod round the cap at the shoulder, and finish its top by cramming or pushing it in where it began. With the shears cut the ends of the nine sticks neat and close, and then proceed with the body case. Cut four sticks about 3 in. longer than the diameter of the bottom of the jar, cut each along the middle of the concave side for 2 in. or 3 in., and tie them exactly as described for the round cob basket in Chapter IV., p. 49, using the butt of the first tie for the half-stick. If osiers are used, the bottom is slewed in the same

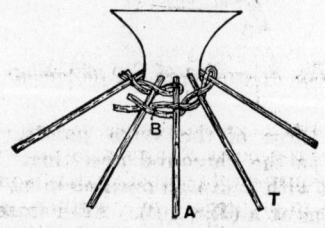

Fig. 102.—Working Strand round Bottle Neck.

way; if very thin cane, it is worked singly, adding another layer in any neat, convenient way when one is finished. When the bottom is paired off, it should be just ½ in. larger than the jar bottom, so that the casing may fit close and neat. Prepare eight pairs of stakes and cut the points on the convex or outer sides, wet them, and, placing the bottom under the left foot, push them in at the right and left of the ends of the sticks. Two of the sticks receive only one stake each, and these should be closer together than the other sticks.

To upset the stakes generally three rods are used, beginning with their butt ends, pointed and driven

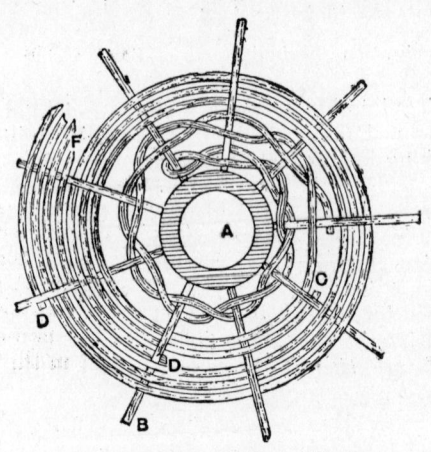

Fig. 103.—Plan of Cap of Casing.

in beside three of the stake points, and then worked as in the three-rod upsetting. When the jar is fitted with a tap an opening must be left for it to enter, as at A (Fig. 104). After upsetting, find the widest space between any two pairs of stakes, and let the projection at the tap-hole A come between them. Now begin the slew as in the round cob basket (Chapter IV.), turning the slew round the stakes D, on either side of the tap-hole, until level with the top of the boss, see Fig. 104, in which C is a single rod, doubled and worked over the boss to receive the odd stake E.

Lap a small osier round the left-hand stake at the tap-hole, so as to make two working strands; twist them over and over each other, and bind the right-hand stake between them, as shown at C

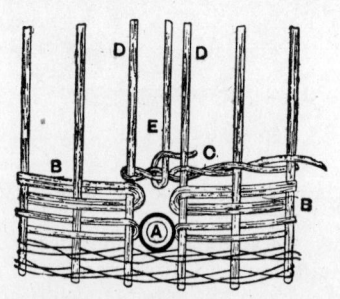

Fig. 104.—Part of Casing showing Tap Opening.

(Fig. 104). Cut the strand and lay it behind a stake, so that it is not noticed. Cut a scallomed stake, as shown in Fig. 105, and scallom it to the twisted rod close to the edge of the boss, as shown at E (Fig. 104). Add another rod butt with the other strand, and continue the slewing round until the

Fig. 105.—Scallomed Rod.

shoulder is reached, where the cap finished. The three-rod slew B (Fig. 104) is kept regular by adding another rod (butt end) on top of the others, just before the top of the bottom rod is finished outside. Simply level the slewing by working a single rod round at the shoulder of the jar. The border must just cover the edge of the cap. Lay down four stakes A, B, C, D (Fig. 106), each behind two others, always working round to the right in bordering; the projecting tops of the four rods are each taken in turn, passed in front of three standing stakes, then behind the fourth, and left in front of the fifth, whilst the last standing stake to

Fig. 106.—Border on Bottle-casing.

the left is laid down beside it. These two actions are repeated right round where the last four or five tops are "crammed" beside those stakes that were first laid down. Cut off neatly the projecting tops of stakes close to the border, and the two handles can then be worked on the border. One rod or cane is generally used for each handle, and, of course, the "cramming" in of the border is always covered with one of the handles; the other is then put on opposite.

Fig. 107.—Handle on Bottle-casing Border.

Cut a point to the butt of each handle-rod as at A (Fig. 107), and push it down from the top of the border beside a stake; now twist it rope-fashion, bend it to the left, and push it under the border in front, using the bodkin, and pull it through from the back; lap it three times over the bow that has been formed, then pass it through the border to the right of its pointed butt end; pull through again, lap it across in the groove, as shown by the dotted line in Fig. 107; return it through the opening at E, and finish at F; cut off neat and close. If worked tightly these single-rod handles often last longer than the case. When very thin cane is used, work it twice under the border C (Fig. 107) instead of returning at E; it must then be finished at B.

In the slewing of these casings it is a good plan to cut the butts of the rods just on the slant by holding a small handful level in the left hand and using the shop-knife; by laying all in with the cut part next to the jar, they will not be so likely to bulge the stakes outwards. Cut off all top ends of the slewing rods outside clean and smooth, and the case is finished. The workman must stand over the jar to work the cap, steadying the jar with his left knee or in any other convenient way.

CHAPTER IX.

DOCTORS' AND CHEMISTS' BASKETS.

A DOCTOR'S or chemist's basket is made by the method about to be described. First cut six sticks each 16 in. long, and put them in a screw block, first putting in the two outer ones at a distance of 8 in. apart, outside measurement. Fill in with weaving for a depth of 13 in., which it is best to mark off with a pencil when beginning the bottom. The method of beginning the filling-in work is described in the chapter on making a grocer's basket, pp. 27 to 30.

Remove the sticks from the block, finish off the work neatly, and cut off the ends of the sticks close. The border inside the basket is 6½ in. deep; ten stakes, say of the thickness of an ordinary lead pencil, will be required for each side, and seven for each end. Cut the butts pointed on the outer or convex side for driving into the bottom. First drive in the end stakes, one at the side of five of the sticks, and two at the third (one each side) from the right hand. When kneeling on the bottom, prick and bend them up. Treat the other end in the same way and pierce the side sticks with the bodkin to receive the ten side stakes. Do not put the outside stakes in the sides too close to the ends as the basket has corner sticks, which greatly add to its appearance. After the ten stakes have been pushed in, prick them up and tap them in close with the flat part of the iron. Do the same with both of the sides; carefully bend the stakes up one at a time and place them in a hoop, lapping a top round the hoop at each side to prevent the latter working off. Cut four sticks about 7 in. long for the corners, and shave a little off at the thin ends to rest against the corners; then proceed with the upsetting by placing the tops of three rods between the stakes in the side, at the left-hand corner, and working in exactly the same manner as for the grocer's square basket already described (see Chapter III.). The stakes should be regulated in upsetting; this applies especially to the two stakes beside the third stick in the ends, so that one may appear as a middle stake. The two stakes at the handle space on each side also should be kept properly apart, and a few minutes spent in

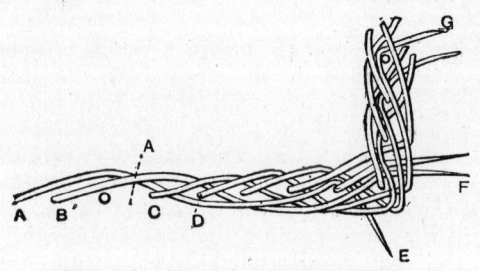

Fig. 108.—Bordering Doctor's Basket.

straightening them after staking the bottom will save much trouble. Two rounds of upsetting can be put on, as they will keep the stakes upright and firm. Take one or two stakes out of the hoop at each side of the four corner sticks, and, after drawing a good double handful of small rods to their different lengths, proceed with the weaving as illustrated by Fig. 41, p. 39. Never weave in rods as thick as the stakes or the work will be a failure. When a depth of about 5½ in. (inside) has been worked all round the wale can be worked on. As the lid of the basket has two flaps, each opening from the end and hinged on a bridge across the handle spaces, the wale can be worked in the same way as the upsetting. One round of six rods is used, the six tops overlapping the entire length of the side where they begin and end. Cut off the ends of the corner sticks and drive a stake in the top of each. Wet the stakes well and commence the border by laying down the third stake in the side and the three following, not counting the left-hand stake in the handle space, which is left standing upright. This border is worked in a similar manner to the foot rim of the grocer's square basket (see p. 29), except that it is close and even. In Fig. 108 the stakes first laid down are shown at A, B, C, and D; E, F, and G are the finished tops of A, B, C; H is the handle space.

When the border is finished a bridge is worked across the width of the basket at the handle spaces. Point the butt ends of two rods and push them down one of the handle spaces as far apart as possible. Then take a weaving-rod, cut a few inches off its top and push it also down the handle space; bring it round the right-hand bridge-rod B (Fig. 109), then between the rods and round the left-hand rod, as illustrated. Work up the rod in this manner, putting its butt end behind one of the bridge rods, as at D (Fig. 109). As each rod is worked up, push in the top end of another, as shown at E, and when sufficient rods have been worked to form the bridge, carefully cut off the butt ends of the weaving-rods close under the bridge. Bend the latter down, bend each of the bridge-rod ends at right angles, point them, and push them down the handle space at the opposite side of the basket; this will form a bridge (Fig. 110) on which the flap lid can be tied. When bending a rod to a sharp angle, as with the bridge-rod ends, always give it a slight twist, which will prevent it breaking. The foot rim is put on next, as described for the square basket in Chapter III. For the flap lids, two rods are bent to the shape of the basket on each side of the bridge; place the butt end of one along the side of the basket, and make two slight notches at the corners. Bend the rod to shape, and tie a strainer across to keep it so, as shown in A (Fig. 111). Cut six

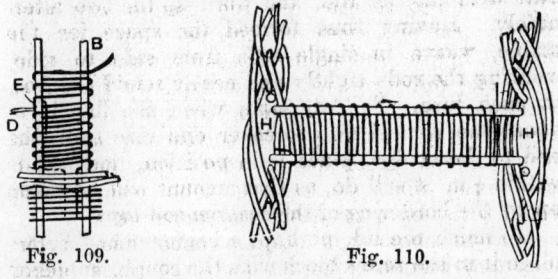

Fig. 109. Fig. 110.

Figs. 109 and 110.—Working Bridge for Doctor's Basket.

scallom-rods (Fig. 112), as shown at B (Fig. 111), and lap them on the bow, in the manner illustrated by Fig. 111. The clear space C is for the staple at each end of the basket. First lap D on the bow, and then E and F; lap the other three rods in the

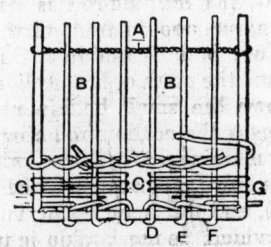

Fig. 111.—Flap Lid for Doctor's Basket.

opposite direction, and weave in some small rods for about three turns at each side of the space, as shown at G. Then work a pair across from the left-hand side of the bow, placing a butt end between the bow and the first scallom-rod; bring the butt tightly round the bow, behind the first scallom, and finish it in front of the second scallom. Now work its top part over it, behind the second and in front of the third scallom, piece the finished butt with another rod, and work up the two alternately. Having thus formed the space for the staple, weave in single rods from side to side, working the rods tightly and neatly round the bow at each turn. To determine when the flap is of about the correct size to cover one side from the end to the bridge, place it in position, and if it is within ¼ in. it will do, as that amount will be taken up by the bordering of the scallom-rod tops.

To finish the lid, perhaps a beginner had better place it in the screw block with the rough, unpicked side facing the worker. Push in a pointed rod beside the bow at the left-hand side; take another small rod, and at about 7 in. from its butt, lap it round the bow and also round the extra stake. Put its butt behind the first scallom-rod, and leave it in front of the second rod where it is finished; the extra stake is then laid down beside it. The other strand of the lapping-rod is passed behind the second scallom and in front of the third, and the first scallom is laid beside it. Repeat these two actions until the sixth or last scallom is reached. Then push down the small bodkin at the side of the bow and pass the scallom-rod that now lies in front of the remaining upright one twice round the bodkin and the bow (to correspond with the opposite side of the lid), and finish by laying it close behind the sixth rod, which, as the bodkin is pulled out, is bent, pointed, and placed in the position of the bodkin. This secures everything, and the lid can be carefully picked and the ends of the bow cut off close as at A (Fig. 113). The other flap is made in exactly the same way, and, when this is done, tie the flaps on each side of the bridge. Pick out four

Doctors' and Chemists' Baskets. 109

long thin rods, point their butts, and use two for each flap. First push in the bodkin beside the bordered scallom D (Fig. 113), wet one of the rods and slip it in the weaving. Hold the flap between the knees, and twist the rod rope fashion; about 4 in. along the weaving, at the right-hand side of the scallom, push in the tip of the twist-rod, pull it through from the back of the flap, and pass it back to the front, at the other side of the same scallom, two strands nearer its starting point. It is then formed as a twist or band, as it is called, by twice lapping it round the 4-in. length, pulling each

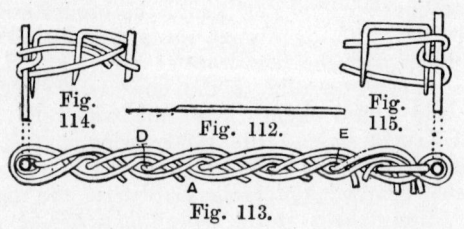

Fig. 112.—Scallom Rod; Fig. 113.—Finishing Lid; Figs. 114 and 115.—Forming Bands for Doctor's Basket.

lap very tightly (see Figs. 114 and 115), then it will appear neat and even as in Figs. 116 and 117, where A represents the border, B the band rod, C the scallom, D the weaving, and E the part used for tying the flap to the bridge. Leave the band whilst working the second rod at E (Fig. 113) in the same way, when the flap can be tied to the bridge. Wet the ends of the twisted rods and place the flap in position, using the bodkin freely when tying. Push the bodkin in the bridge weaving, insert the end of the twisted rod and pull it from inside the basket through the flap to the outside (tightly), and again through the bridge up through the flap. It is then worked in its groove, in the original twist or band, and cut off outside, where the band rod first went through the weaving. The three other tie-rods are worked in the same way at their respective positions (see Fig. 118), where A is one of the bridge sticks, B the lid border, and C the finished end of the band.

For the bow and skein handle, first cut two small sticks to form the bow, and place them side by side in the handle spaces H (Fig. 110, p. 107), bending one at a time, of course. Be sure that they are perfectly level at the shoulder bends. The highest part of the bow sticks may be about 8 in., or any other desirable height from the bridge. Cut a scallomed rod and push its cut part under the border in front of the bow, and up through the top of the border, in contact with the bow front at Figs. 119 and 120, where A is the border, B the bow, C the scallam-rod, and D the skein. Push the wide end of a soaked skein behind the bows, bring it over the border at the left-hand side, pass it over the scallom-rod, and under the border at the right; then bring it over at the same side, cross it over, and pass it under the border at the left side. Again bring it over the front and lap it round the bows and scallom-rod six or seven times, working upwards; then pass the skein behind the scallom-rod, as shown at E (Fig. 120). After lapping the bows and scallom together for three turns, again pass them under the scallom once, and so on. About 3 in. or 4 in. from the finishing side the scallom-rod must be twisted rope fashion and pushed under the border in front; then pull it up tightly beside the bows, to correspond with the beginning. Proceed by lapping all the bows, etc., close, and finish off, to correspond with the other side, by pulling the skein between the scallom and border once or twice and cutting it off; then it will be quite secure. As the handle will take several skeins, the piecing is shown in Fig. 121. The end A is pointed, and pushed in the lapping under the bows for about 2 in. at 2 in. from the end of a finished skein B. Bend both at right angles, as shown, the skein A taking the place of B, and bind the latter firmly out of sight.

The bows should be pegged by piercing through the wale in a line with the border and just under it, at both sides of the basket. A pointed short

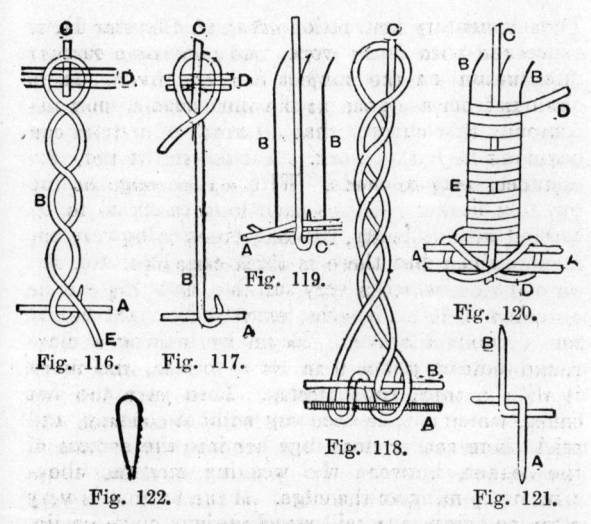

Figs. 116 to 118.—Forming Bands for Doctor's Basket; Figs. 119 and 120.—Lapping Handle; Fig. 121.—Piecing Skeins; Fig. 122.—Staple.

piece of rod is tapped in and cut off slanting so as not to catch in anything. The staples are pieces of rod bent closely round the bodkin as shown in Fig. 122; put them in the basket ends so that they project through the space in the flap-lid, and use the bodkin to get them in the border, one on each end, at the middle stake, finally pushing them down and pegging them.

CHAPTER X.

FANCY BASKETS.

THE elementary instruction given in Chapter II. is concerned with fancy work, and now some further information on the subject can be given. It is obvious from a glance at the illustrations that accompany this chapter that all kinds of articles can be made in basket-work. A rubbish basket, for instance, may be made. With a rope edge at the top this basket requires such long canes as to be worked with difficulty, the long canes being very unmanageable; but there is thick cane (No. 16), flat on one side, which is very suitable, and this can be obtained in 10 in. lengths, exactly the right height for a rubbish basket. Begin by making a close round bottom about 9 in. in diameter, and finish it with a thick rope edging. Then take the flat canes, which can be used dry without soaking, and stick them rather close together into the bottom of the basket, between the weaving strands, about 1 in. or 1½ in. from the edge. If the bottom is very close and firm they will stand upright quite easily, and after a few rows of weaving they will be as firm as possible. The bottom of the basket, being damp, will shrink in drying, and hold the uprights quite tightly. Weave the sides of the basket as usual till within 2 in. of the top; then cut pieces of No. 8 cane long enough to make the rope edging, and push them down about 1 in. by the side of each upright. Weave to the very top of the uprights, then use the No. 8 stakes for the rope-twist. It is a little monotonous to weave a whole rubbish basket alike all the way up, but variety can be introduced easily. Weave, say, 2 in. in the usual way; then introduce a second strand, and weave another 2 in. with two strands together, one above the other; then do another band of plain weaving, and so on. Or there is another material known as "insides" or "flat pulp." This makes a nice variety, woven in alternate bands with the round cane. It is to be had in two widths, $\frac{1}{8}$ in. or $\frac{1}{4}$ in. wide, Nos. 40 and 50. It can also be had in black, but the black dye

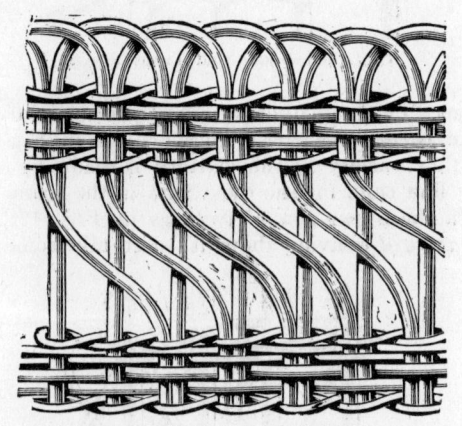

Fig. 123.—Open-work Design.

comes off on the hands. Straw plait woven in gives variety, or plaited chip, which can be had in all colours at kindergarten shops. Green rush plait also can be used.

Open-work patterns are effective, and one is shown by Fig. 123. Work as usual till the sides of the basket are about 1 in. high, then finish off with a row of twist (Fig. 25, p. 20). Leave a space of about an inch (or more if a big basket), and begin again with a row of twist; to do this measure on a weaving strand rather more than the circumfer-

H

ence of the basket, double the strand at that distance from the end, loop it round an upright, and work the twist as before (Fig. 124), fasten off the short end when the row is finished, and continue weaving with the long end. Having finished the basket, bend over the stakes for a "trellis-work"

Fig. 124.—Spoke and Twist Design.

edging; but instead of pushing them straight down make them cross the open space, as in Fig. 123. Another variety of this pattern is made by using very fine cane for the cross bars in the open part. Work the upper row of twist as in Fig. 124, and two rows of weaving above it; then take some very

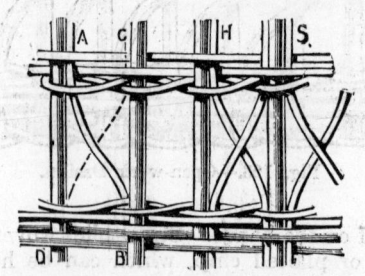

Fig. 125.—Crossed Open-work Design.

fine cane—say No. 00—push in one piece at A (Fig. 125), take it across the open space, and push it down at B. Then put in another piece at C, take it across to D, thus making a crossways pattern in each open space, as shown at H in Fig. 125. Repeat this in each space, or in alternate spaces, all round the basket. If long ends are left of the fine cane, each of the original uprights will have a fine cane on each side of it, as at s. Continue weaving to the top of the basket, treating each group as though it were only one upright, and this will hold the fine cane firmly. To finish the basket, make a twist outside, using only the original thick canes (the thin ones can be curled round inside the basket to be out of the way), and when that

Fig. 126.—Zigzag Pattern.

is done, make a twist inside the basket of the fine canes; this makes a pretty double border.

A great variety of fancy patterns can be made in the style illustrated by Fig. 126. It looks best to have a large number of uprights very close together, and to use a double strand for weaving. For the pattern shown at Fig. 126 the number of uprights must be divisible by twelve, that being the number required for each repetition of the pattern. The pattern is really all alike in each row—over four, under one, over three; under one, over one, under four. In the second row this is repeated, only beginning one upright more to the right, and so on till it is time to turn; then work the next row one spoke to the left, and each row one more to the left, so that the pattern will go in zigzags. Fig. 126 explains this more clearly than any written description can.

Knitting patterns will often suggest ideas for this kind of "fancy stitch," and cross-stitch patterns of a simple kind also can be worked out in fine weaving.

Fig. 127.—Sewing.

The lid of a fancy basket is like the bottom, the weaving being pulled rather tight to make the lid slightly hollow; but a lid will not fit neatly on a twisted edge, therefore both the top of the basket and the edge of the lid should be finished with a flat binding. Some use "pink tie" for binding, this being the cane used for chair seats, shiny on one side; but the shiny surface is apt to flake off, and it is always a darker colour than the basket. A far nicer material is the "insides" or "flat pulp" mentioned before; it is the same colour as the round cane, but flat. To bind a basket, finish the weaving with a row of twist (Fig. 25, p. 20), and cut off the uprights close above it. Cut two pieces of the flat cane to the measurement of the circumference of the basket, and hold them face to face, one on each side of the uprights. Then, with a longer piece of the flat stuff, sew them tightly round the basket by pushing one end of the sewing piece through the side of the basket about two strands from the top, then over both the binding pieces and again through the basket, exactly like ordinary sewing. About two stitches between each spoke will be found the best, as the sewing should be done close. The binding pieces must be pulled tight as the sewing goes on. Fig. 127 helps to

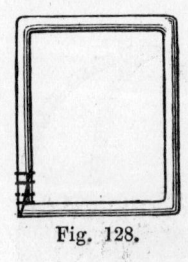

Fig. 128.

Figs. 128 and 129.—Basket Frame.

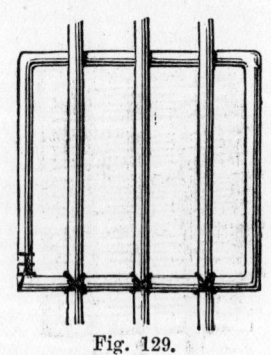

Fig. 129.

explain the sewing. The edge of the lid should be bound in exactly the same way, and should be made a trifle larger than the top of the basket. It can easily be fastened on with a piece of the sewing material for a hinge. A glance at any basket with a lid will show how this is done. Readers who have mastered the more useful and practical work described in former chapters will have no difficulty here.

One kind of square or oblong fancy basket is made on a frame of thick cane (No. 8 or No. 9). Bend it into a square by pinching the corners, and tie the ends, which should overlap, with thin string, as in Fig. 128.

Cut the uprights as usual, long enough to go down one side of the basket, across the square bottom, and up the other side, and tie them with string to the bottom of the frame, leaving the other ends free (Fig. 129). With a No. 3 cane weave backwards and forwards across the frame, taking in the sides of the frame also. After a few rows of weaving insert a cane right across, long enough for the sides of the basket; weave a few more rows and insert another long cane, and so on at even distances till

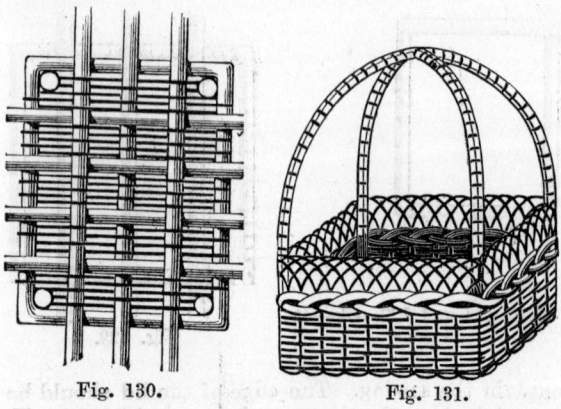

Fig. 130.   Fig. 131.

Fig. 130.—Bottom of Oblong Basket; Fig. 131.—Square Fancy Basket.

the frame is quite filled. Then cut away the string, and this square piece will be the bottom of the basket (Fig. 130).

The sides can now be turned up, not over the frame, but away from it, and a thick stake must be stuck upright in the very corner of the frame, as shown by the white circles in the corners of Fig. 130. The canes may be turned quite upright or sloping outwards, according to the shape required. Straight sides are the easier.

The weaving is done just as in a round fancy basket, only pinching the weaving-strand at each corner when it comes outside the thick spoke, to make the corners sharp. As there is an even number of spokes, two weaving-strands must be used; one had better be rolled up, or they will get very much entangled. When the sides are done, the loose sides of the frame should be sewn to the basket to make a neat finish. See Fig. 127, p. 116, for the way to do the sewing.

An uncommon kind of square fancy basket is illustrated by Fig. 131. It must be made in tolerably fine cane, say No. 1, of which a large quantity will be required. The uprights are all of the fine cane; they must be cut very long, and arranged as in Fig. 132. The crossway canes, in groups of six, should be laid on a table, with weights at each end to keep them steady. Then the longway canes, in groups of three, are threaded in and out, and pushed quite close together, while the crossway canes remain at some distance apart. A string tied across each end will be found a great help in arranging this; it can be cut away afterwards.

With two weaving-strands of No. 1 cane make a row of twist all round to keep it all together; but as there are too many uprights at the ends, each pair of bundles must be overlapped and used as one group; this being shown at the upper end of Fig. 132. This helps to make the uprights firm; but if it seems clumsy, some of them may be cut short. The side canes, on the contrary, are much too far apart, therefore more groups of six must be inserted at A, B, and C on each side, as shown in the diagram, Fig. 132. There will be difficulty in getting all this fixed. However, when it has been done, weave round and round, keeping the work flat on a table till it is the right size for the bottom of the basket. Two or three rows of twist may be done before the weaving; it helps to keep everything in its place.

Turn up the sides as usual (they will come up best if a binding is sewn round the bottom, as in Fig. 127, p. 116), and stick in a short thick stake of No. 8 cane at each corner. Weave as usual, pinching the corners whilst weaving till the basket is about two-thirds of the required height, and finish the weaving as usual with a row of twist. Now there are numerous uprights in groups of six. Divide each group in half, and use three at a time for a looped edging, with a broad flat plait below it (Fig. 131). Take a group of three uprights, bend them to the right, and pass them behind three groups, in front of two groups, behind two groups, in front of two groups, and behind one group, the ends now coming down outside the basket. Always remember that each group now consists of only three uprights, so that each large set must be divided as the worker proceeds.

Continue this all round, taking each set of three uprights behind 3, in front of 2, behind 2, in front of 2, and out behind 1. When this is done all round, pull down the uprights till the edge is quite even all round, and then make the plait. Take each upright in turn, and pass it under two to the right. Do this all round, and the ends will now all be pointing upwards, still outside the basket. Pull them all as tight as they will conveniently go, and get them even all round. Now again pass each upright under 2, downwards to the right; pull them tight all round, and the plait should lie flat against the basket just below the looped edging, with the ends pointing downwards. When dry, cut off the ends in the middle of the plait as close as possible.

A handle may be made of two long pieces of No. 8 cane, closely bound round with the flat "insides," or with "pink tie." Fasten one end firmly in one corner, and the other end in the **opposite corner** diagonally across the basket. Pre-

FANCY BASKETS. 121

pare another similar handle, and fasten it in the other two corners, making it cross the first handle in the middle, where the two must be fastened together.

An effective way of binding a handle is to place two or three lengths of thick cane side by side;

Fig. 132.—Weaving Square Fancy Basket.

wind round with "insides," or "pink tie," say, five times; then push the binding-piece under one of the foundation pieces, and bind only two together for three stitches. Then wind over all the pieces five stitches more, and repeat this for the whole length (Fig. 133).

Oval baskets can be made with a foundation

adapted from Fig. 132, with six or eight long-way pieces, of No. 3 cane, and six sets of three for crossway spokes, the weaving being done with No. 1 or No. 0. This avoids a raised ridge.

Dolls' furniture in basket-work is made with fine cane, unless the articles are to be of large size.

For a doll's garden chair (Fig. 134) use No. 4 cane for uprights, and No. 0 for weaving. The seat is done first, on a square frame (Fig. 128, p. 117), the back end being a trifle narrower than the front. Having filled the frame, turn up the thicker canes and weave a few rows, about six, finishing with a row of twist. Leave a space, begin again with a row of twist, weave six more rows, and finish off by bending each of the spokes in turn behind one, in

Fig. 133.—Handle for Fancy Basket.

front of one, behind one, in front of one, behind one. All the ends are now inside, and can be cut off. This is the base of the chair. Stand it down with the seat uppermost. Now put in stakes for the arms and back, by pushing them down into the upper rows of weaving on three sides of the seat, leaving the front open. Weave a few rows backwards and forwards, turning back when the last spoke is reached. After a few rows finish with a row of twist; leave a space and begin weaving again, to match the base. Make another narrow band of weaving as shown in Fig. 134, leave a second space, and then bend over the spokes to finish the top. This should be done higher at the back than in front. Each spoke goes behind one, in front of two, behind one, in front of one, behind one. This must be done on each side, starting from the opposite ends, so as to make the two sides match, and the middle spokes must be pushed in anywhere to make a neat finish. Of course, both the base and back could be done entirely in close weaving if preferred, but leaving spaces as described makes the chair look lighter.

Another kind of doll's chair is shown by Fig. 135. Begin with a round flat piece as for an ordinary basket. When it is large enough for the seat of the chair, turn up the uprights and weave the sides, drawing the weaving tighter and tighter till the uprights are quite close together; then gradually

Fig. 134.    Fig. 135.

Fig. 134.—Doll's Garden Chair; Fig. 135.—Doll's Round Chair.

spread them again until the shape resembles an hour-glass, and finish off with a rope edge. This makes a capital round stool, but to make it into a chair it must have a back. Run in new stakes for the back, either flat into the seat or perpendicular into the sides, leaving a space for the front, and weave backwards and forwards for the sides and back. The back is made higher by putting in more rows of weaving. When the sides are high enough, leave out the first upright on each side; in the next row leave out two uprights on each side, and so on till the back slopes up nicely. Finish with a rope edge, or any other preferred.

For a doll's cradle (Fig. 136) make a shallow oval basket, having the uprights at one end much longer than the rest to form the hood. Turn up the sides, and finish with a trellis-work edge drawn close down upon the weaving. This edge must not be done all round; the part for the hood must be left, and the weaving continued. For the hood, weave backwards and forwards a few rows; then work as shown in Fig. 137 in order to raise the weaving higher in the middle. Work a few rows plain, all across, and again raise the middle, repeating this till the hood is sufficiently large. Bend the front spoke on the

Fig. 136.—Doll's Cradle.

right across the front of the hood and push it down by the side of the front spoke on the left. Take the left front spoke and push it down in the same way on the opposite side; this makes a good firm rim for the hood. Each remaining spoke must be turned over this front rim and pushed back upon itself to make a neat edge.

A doll's table can be made like Fig. 138. The top is a round flat piece, finished with a rope edge. For the legs take two pieces of cane, No. 4 or 5, and having made the middle of the table as in Fig. 139, push in one end of one piece at the opening, A, and the other end at B. In the same way push down the second piece at C and D, pulling the four ends down underneath the table till the top is quite flat.

FANCY BASKETS.

Each of these ends must be twice the height of the table. Turn the table upside down with the legs pointing upwards, and weave a few rows to spread

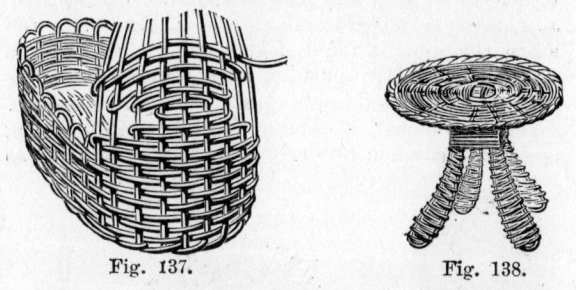

Fig. 137.

Fig. 138.

Fig. 137.—Hood of Cradle; Fig. 138.- Doll's Table.

them outwards. The best way is to twist the weaving strand right round each upright in turn, and three or four rows of this will be sufficient. Or

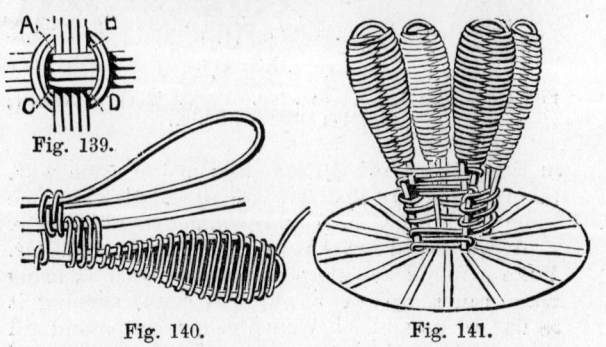

Fig. 139.

Fig. 140.

Fig. 141.

Figs. 139 to 141.—Constructing Doll's Table.

another way is to weave backwards and forwards three rows between spokes 1 and 2; repeat the same between spokes 2 and 3, then between 3 and 4, then between 4 and 1. Each leg is finished separately, and to do this, double one spoke into a loop of the length required for the height of the table, cut it, and push the end into the weaving just done; then weave backwards and forwards, filling up the loop as closely as possible, as shown in Fig. 140; and when the loop is filled, fasten off the end of the weaving strand by pushing it in somewhere. The loop must be filled much closer than is illustrated; it is drawn loosely worked to show how the weaving is done, but when properly filled it must appear as

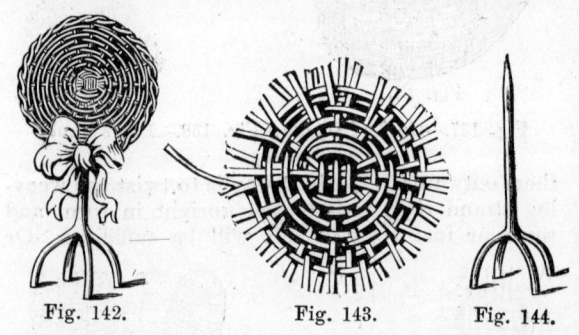

Fig. 142.   Fig. 143.   Fig. 144.

Fig. 142.—Fire Screen; Fig. 143.—Basket Work of Screen; Fig. 144.—Screen Stand.

in Fig. 141. Work all four legs in the same way, taking great care that they are all exactly the same height, as otherwise the table will not stand steadily.

A fire-screen for real use is shown by Fig. 142. Make a round flat piece of weaving with as many main canes as can be worked with, keeping it as flat as possible. Weave round and round till the radials or thicker canes get too far apart, and when that happens, push in stakes, as shown in Fig. 143, one on each side of each of the radials. Fig. 143 shows how thirteen radials have been increased to thirty-seven. Go on weaving, still keeping it quite flat, till more stakes are required. Insert these again in the same way, and so continue till there is a flat circular piece 2 ft. or more in diameter. Finish this with a thick rope edge, as firmly as possible. An iron stand resembling Fig. 144 will have to be made. Push the long spike of the stand right up into the weaving as far as the middle; this should be done before the rope edge is made, so that the rope holds it quite tight. Paint the iron stand to match the basket-work, or else cover it entirely with "flat pulp" wound closely

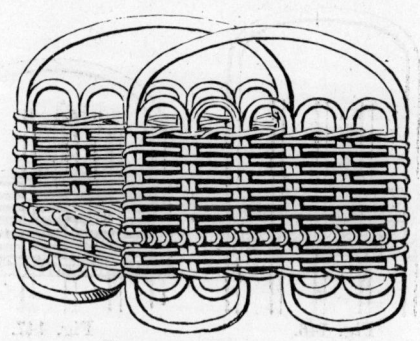

Fig. 145.—Paper Rack.

round it. Finish off with a bow of ribbon, as suggested in Fig. 142. If the iron rod is rather thick and cannot be pushed in, one or more of the spokes can be cut close to the middle and pulled out, and the iron inserted in the space thus made. This screen stands on the floor. Hand-screens can be made in much the same way, with black and gold handles, which can be bought for a small sum.

In making a paper rack, Fig. 145, begin with the flat bottom on which the papers stand. This is made on a rectangular frame, like the bottom of a square basket (see Fig. 128, p. 117). Fill the frame by weaving backwards and forwards; and to finish off the thicker canes fold them over the frame at the ends, and run them back into the weaving. No cross canes are required. When the bottom is done, push through it at one side a sufficient number of stakes, as in Fig. 146, but preferably there should be an even number. The end stakes must be one piece of cane bent over: this makes the handle; the others are single pieces (see Fig. 147). Now weave the side, backwards and forwards, to the height required, and finish with a looped edge, as shown in

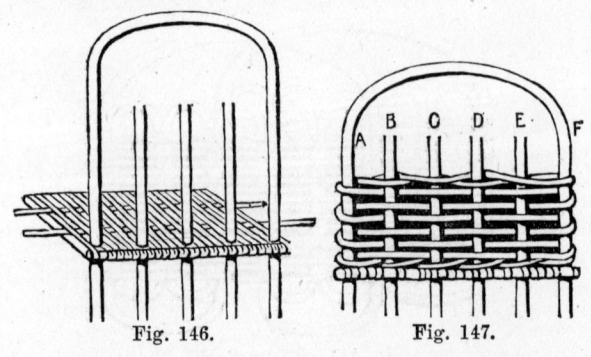

Fig. 146.   Fig. 147.

Figs. 146 and 147.—Constructing Paper Rack.

Fig. 145. Stake B, Fig. 147, is pushed down by the side of A, C by B, D by C, E by D; then a false spoke must be added to make the loop between E and F. Work the other side of the rack exactly to match.

Turn the whole thing upside down, and weave a few rows for the band below the bottom, to make it steady. This also is to be finished with a looped edge, as illustrated, both sides alike.

If the rack is to have a division in the middle, stakes must be pushed through in the middle of the bottom, and a piece worked exactly like the sides. It will be easier to do this first and the sides afterwards. A piece below the bottom should also be

FANCY BASKETS.

woven at the two ends, to hold the sides upright. Push both ends of a stake downwards through the bottom, and draw them down tightly; each piece of cane will thus make two stakes.

If the rack is a large one, the handle can be made much thicker by inserting two extra pieces of cane by the side of it and binding the three together, as in Fig. 148, with either "pink tie" or "flat pulp."

Variety can be given by making a close bottom

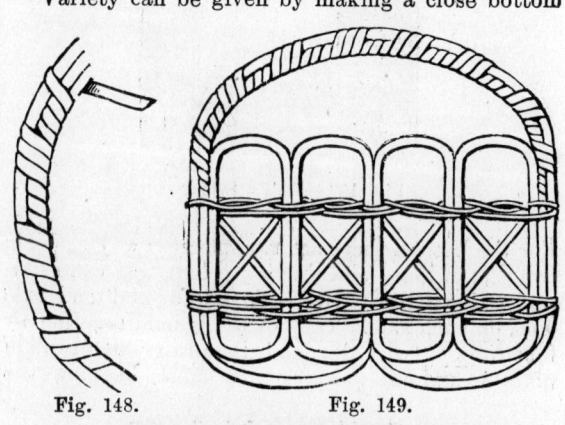

Fig. 148.   Fig. 149.

Fig. 148.—Paper Rack Handle; Fig. 149.—Open-work Side for Paper Rack.

and open-work sides to the paper-rack. This could be lined with bright-coloured material (see Fig. 149).

A doll's bedstead (Fig. 150) can be made very much like a miniature paper-rack, the ends instead of the sides being woven, and one end being higher than the other, for the head of the bed; with a little ingenuity the same plan could be adapted easily in making a sofa, by weaving the two ends and the back. A plain chair could also be made in the same way, with a square seat, omitting the upper part of the footboard.

A Madeira oval open-work basket (Fig. 151) is made on much the same plan as that described for the square fancy basket, pp. 119 to 121. The whole basket should be made in the very finest cane, No. 00.

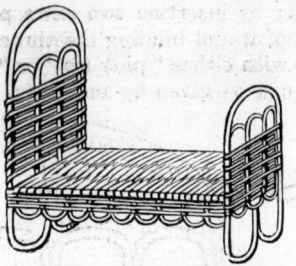

Fig. 150.—Doll's Bedstead.

For the bottom there are twenty cross-way canes in five sets of four; and thirty-two long-way canes, arranged in six sets of two in the middle and ten single ones on each side. The bottom is held together by four rows of twist all round, then thirty-two rows of plain in-and-out weaving are done, keeping the

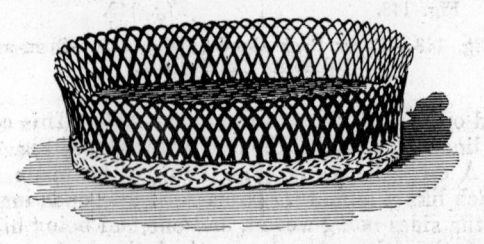

Fig. 151.—Madeira Open-work Basket.

principal canes divided into groups of four. This makes a flat oval bottom about 7½ in. by 5½ in. Push in extra stakes about 20 in. long, always in sets of four, one set among each set of the principal canes,

FANCY BASKETS.   131

and one set in each space between (cutting the original canes off short) till there are fifty-six groups of four strands each. Turn these up at right angles to the flat bottom. There is no plain weaving at the sides, the open-work beginning at once (see Fig. 152).

Take each group of four uprights in turn to the right, in front of three groups, behind two, in front of two, behind two, and bring the ends down outside the basket. Go all round like this, threading in and out by the same rule, and return to the starting point.

Fig. 152.—Side of Madeira Basket.

Pull all the ends till the border has an even height of 2 in. all round. The ends are all outside, pointing downwards. For the plait, which also makes a little rim for the basket to stand on, take each set of four stakes in turn and pass it to the right in front of two groups, behind two, and leave the ends pointing upwards. Get this even all round. Then take each set again to the right, in front of two groups, and behind one, the ends now all pointing downwards. Having got this even all round, cut off the ends an inch or two from the basket; let it get quite dry, and then cut them close in the middle of the plait. If the basket is not quite dry before the final cutting, the ends will shrink and the plait come undone.

CHAPTER XI.

SUSSEX TRUG BASKETS.

The Sussex trug basket is made of very thin wood instead of osiers, and was first made in Sussex; even now, it is believed, they are not made outside a radius of ten miles of the original manufactory, which is a matter for surprise. The uses to which they can be put are legion; the larger sizes are used in breweries, coal-yards, timber-yards, gardens, and in many other places; while the smaller sizes find a large sale at seaside towns for children; ornamental kinds are used largely as ladies' work-baskets, flower-pots, etc. They are very durable, and, if not allowed to be continually wet, they will last a lifetime.

The principal tool used in making Sussex trugs is the drawing-knife, known also as the draw-shave; this will have to be bought. Other necessary tools are a hand-saw, small axe, cleaving axe, hammer, and an old flat-iron; further appliances required can be made by the worker himself.

The most useful of these home-made appliances is the shaving-horse, shown in side view by Fig. 153 and in end view by Fig. 154. To make this, get a plank about 6 ft. long and from 10 in. to 12 in. wide, and about 6 in. from each end bore two $1\frac{1}{4}$-in. holes, and drive a leg in each, to form a stool as high as a chair; the legs must spread well, so as to make the bench firm. Get two pieces of ash or similar wood, 2 ft. 6 in. long, and about 3 in. by $1\frac{1}{2}$ in., and in each piece bore two $1\frac{1}{4}$-in. holes 6 in. from each end, and a $\frac{3}{4}$-in. hole 13 in. from the top end; these pieces are marked D in Figs. 153 and 154. Two round pieces fit the largest holes, one (E) 3 in. longer than the stool is wide, and the other (H) 12 in. longer. These must be driven tightly into the side pieces, to form a frame which will easily slip on the stool. Bore a

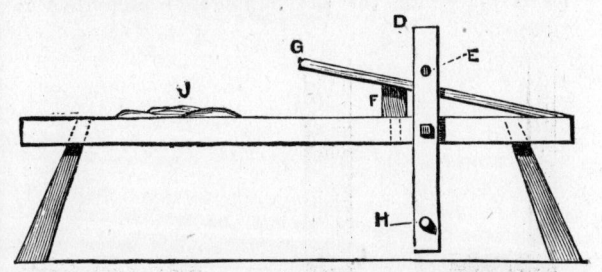

Fig. 153.—Side Elevation of Shaving-horse.

¾-in hole through the stool edgeways, 1 ft. 9 in. from one end, and, putting the frame on, pass a bolt (I) through the sides of the frame and through the stool. There now is a stool with a frame swinging on it. The longer round piece should be at the bottom, and should project 4½ in. at each side. A block of wood,

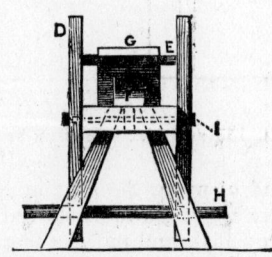

Fig. 154.—End Elevation of Shaving-horse.

10 in. long and about 4 in. wide by 3 in. thick (see F), must be fixed in the centre of stool, an inch or two nearer the long end than the bolt, I. To fix F, tenon it through the top of stool and pin it. Cut off the

134   BASKET WORK.

block on the bevel as illustrated, so that a board G, which is 6 in. wide, will bed on top of it; fix this board to the short end of the bench. Fig. 153 explains what is meant. A cushion (J) upon which to sit is placed on the shaving-horse, which then is complete.

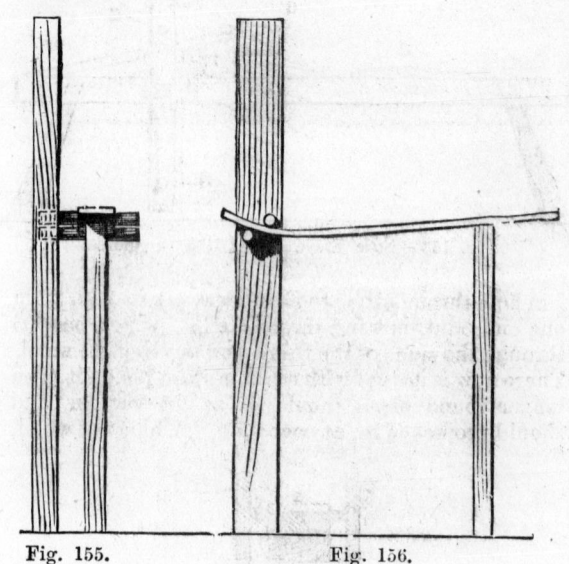

Fig. 155.   Fig. 156.

Figs. 155 and 156.—Shaving-brake.

The method of using the shaving-horse is to sit astride it, place the wood to be shaved on the board G (Figs. 153 and 154), and put the feet, one on each side, on the projecting pieces H, thrusting them forward; the frame swings on the bolt I, and clips the wood between the board G and the round piece E; the more pressure required on the work the more are the feet thrust forward. This shaving-horse is a very useful appliance in any wood-working shop.

The whole of the wood for the smaller trugs can be prepared on the shaving-horse; but the rims and handles for the larger sizes are prepared on the shaving-brake, shown in end view by Fig. 155 and in side view by Fig. 156. This simply is a stump driven in the ground and two pegs inserted in it, one a trifle higher than the other. The piece to be

Fig. 157.—Steaming Trough.

shaved has its end put between the two pegs, its other end being bent up to the top of a shorter stump, when the spring of the wood will hold it firmly. Fig. 156 makes the arrangement clear. The pegs should be about 4 ft. from the ground; that also is the height from the ground of the shorter stump.

A steam trough for steaming the rims and handles, to make them bend easily, will be required only by those who go in for the largest sizes, or make in a large way to sell again. It may be fitted up in connection with the ordinary washing copper. In Fig. 157 L is the copper, M the fire, O the chimney, P the stokehole, Q a support for the end of trough K, which is a watertight box about 6 ft. long and 9 in. square, stopped at the end nearest the chimney, and

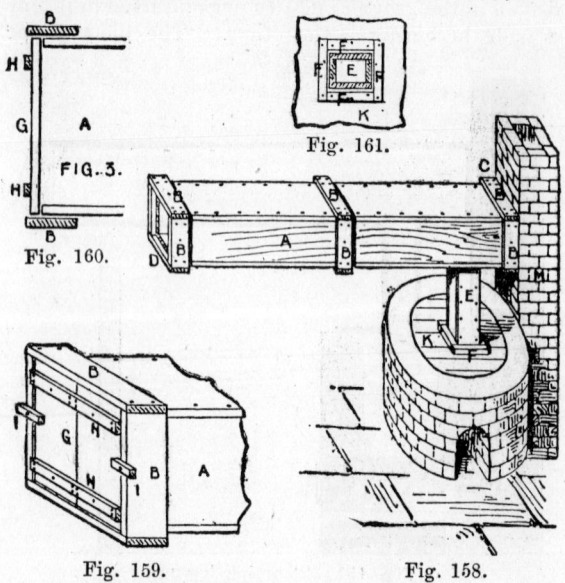

Fig. 158.—Steaming Apparatus; Figs. 159 and 160.—End of Steam Trough; Fig. 161.—Attachment of Steam Tube to Copper.

fitted with a movable lid at R; a square tube N leads from the copper to the trough, and it is understood easily that when the trough K is filled with the pieces of wood, the door R closed firmly, and the water kept boiling for half an hour, the wood will be steamed well, and will then bend without difficulty. The smaller pieces of wood can be boiled in water, in which case a trough is not required.

Details of the steaming apparatus may be given for the benefit of those who intend to work in a large way.

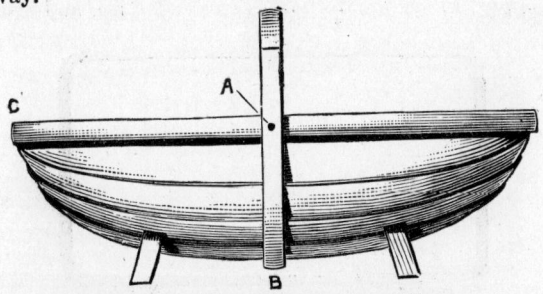

Fig. 162.—Front View of Sussex Trug.

The steam trough proper (A, Figs. 158 to 161) is a square box about 6 ft. long, made from four 9-in. by 1-in. boards, and strengthened as at B. The end C (Fig. 158) is closed up, but at the end D the strengthening pieces project about 1½ in. beyond the trough so as to form a rebate. All round, in this rebate,

Fig. 163.—End View of Sussex Trug.

a door, G, is fitted, and held in place by a button, I, on each side, as shown in Fig. 159. The door is strengthened by ledges, H. The trough is connected

138 BASKET WORK.

with the copper by means of the wooden pipe E, which fits in a socket formed by nailing four cleats, F, on to bottom side of trough, and also on lid of copper, K. A square hole is cut in the lid, and also

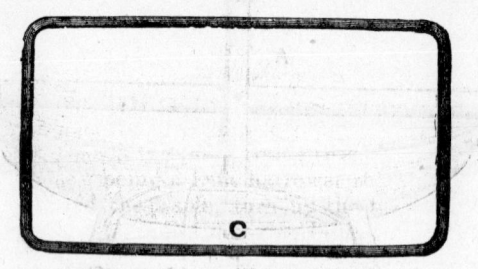

Fig. 164.—Rim of Sussex Trug.

in the trough, for the steam to pass through. The trough is fixed in a horizontal position, the pipe E supporting the end C, while the other end can be suspended from the roof or propped from the floor, as most convenient (see Fig. 157). Fig. 158 is an elevation of steam trough attached to set pan; Fig. 159,

Fig. 166.

Fig. 165.

Fig. 165.—Handle of Sussex Trug; **Fig. 166.**—Foot of Sussex Trug.

elevation of end, showing movable door; Fig. 160, vertical section through end and door; Fig. 161, plan of attachment of steam tube to copper lid.

A Sussex trug basket is shown in side view by Fig. 162 and in end view by Fig. 163, and from these it will be seen to consist of four parts—the rim (Fig. 164), the handle (Fig. 165), the feet (Fig. 166), and the boards (Fig. 167). The rims and handles are made of ash or chestnut poles about 2 in. in diameter, the straightest material and that most clear from knots being most suitable; these should be cut to lengths and quartered, that is, cleft through the middle and then cleft at right angles to the first cleaving, thus producing four pieces in section like Fig. 168. Shave off the sharp angle at the pith, trim

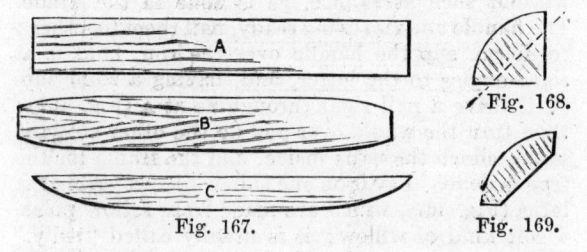

Fig. 167.—Boards of Sussex Trug; Figs. 168 and 169.— Sections of Rim of Sussex Trug.

off any irregularities left from cleaving, and just take off all sharp edges, the section then resembling Fig. 169. The less the outside is touched the better, because strength is wanted there in bending. The ends for about 6 in. must be thinned down, so that two ends may come together and form a neat joint, about the same thickness as the rest of the rim. The handles are made in exactly the same way. The shaving being done, the wood is steamed or boiled, and then the putting together can be proceeded with. This the beginner will manage best by making a board of the same shape as a rim. In making a trug about 15 in. by 8 in., a board is required ½ in. less each way than this, with the corners rounded off;

bend the rim round the edge of the board, and fasten the splicing with three or four nails. The splicing should be in the middle of the long side, as at C (Fig. 164). The handle will be managed in the same way, only, of course, the board will have to be the shape of Fig. 165; and as the handle is nailed on outside the rim, the inside measurement of the handle will have to be as much as the outside measurement of the rim, though this need not be exact, as they will yield one to another. After some practice the workman will learn to dispense with the boards altogether, and bend both handles and rims without such assistance, as is done in the trade. The handle and rim being ready, nail them together; to do so, slip the handle over the rim, hold it at right angles to the latter, and, having a solid support, drive a nail right through as at A (Fig. 162); then turn the whole over and do the other side the same, clinch the nails inside, and the frame for the trug is done. Lay it on one side while preparing the laths (Fig. 167), which are made from sallow poles, a soft kind of willow; it is usually called "sally." The poles are cut off to the lengths required for the various sizes; the trug of the size mentioned above will require boards 21 in. long. The wood is cleft as thin as possible—the thinner the better—as there is then less shaving to do. After cleaving out with the cleaving axe, lay them in a pile by the side of the shaving-horse, so that they can be reached without the worker moving from his seat; shave one side plain, and do the other side the same, but a trifle round, so as to make them thinnest at the edges; then turn ends and do the same again, the lath then being finished. Boards can be made to any of the shapes shown in Fig. 167, whichever will suit best, and they will all come in. In putting the bottom in the trug, select a lath resembling A (Fig. 167), press it down in the framework, and drive a nail into the handle at B (Fig. 162); bend the lath to the shape there shown, and nail again at C. Do the other end the same, and the first lath is fixed, as one nail at each place is enough. Take a lath something like B (Fig. 167), and proceed in the same way, just allowing it to lap over the edge of the first one, and so proceed on each side from the centre till the trug is finished. The last lath on each side will resemble C (Fig. 167), and will most likely require fitting a little to the rim, which is best done with a sharp knife; the knife also is used for trimming off ends of laths after they are nailed in. It will be found that it takes about seven laths to complete the job, though, if they are of a good width, five will do it, and again, if very narrow, it will require more; but there should always be an odd number—that is, there should be an equal number on each side of the centre one.

The feet, Fig. 166, p. 138, now have to be made and put on. They can be made from any odds and ends of wood, and are about 1 in. thick. They are nailed through from the inside.

A cleaving axe is mentioned above; this is shown by Fig. 170, in which A is the wooden handle, B is the blade, and C the eye of the blade in which the handle is fixed; D is a plan of the blade looking at the bottom. To use it, the piece of wood to be cleft is stood on one end, and the edge laid on it where it is to be split, the handle being held upright in the left hand; the blade is struck on the thick part with a billet of wood until it is well in, when the handle is used as a lever and at once splits the wood. The proper nails to use are the stout wire ones with large flat heads, and they are clinched on the flat-iron before mentioned; they can be driven in fearlessly, as there is no fear of splitting the wood.

The walking-stick basket (Fig. 171) is simply a combination of the trug with a walking-stick, and made very simply. First make the trug part, as already described; it must be about 8 in. in diameter each way. The stick is a straight piece of ash, the crook on the top being formed by steaming and bending in the same way as the rims and handles; cut a hole in the bottom of the trug, so that the stick will go just through. Get two turned collars, as shown in plan and sectional elevation by Fig. 172, and fix one of these on the stick, about 6 in. below the crook;

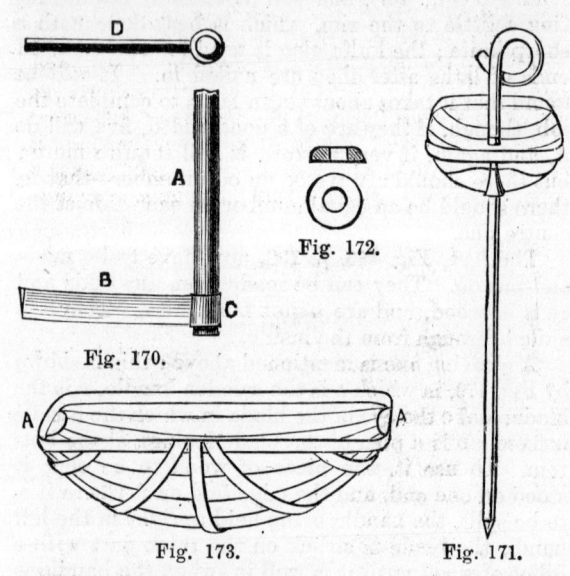

Fig. 170.—Cleaving Axe; Fig. 171.—Walking-stick Basket; Fig. 172.—Collar for Walking-stick Basket; Fig. 173.—Caul, or Wood Basket.

then pass the stick through the hole in the bottom of the trug, so that the collar fits in the trug; slip the second collar on the stick, and fix up close to the trug with a small nail; then the walking-stick basket is complete.

This basket is sold very largely in places frequented by tourists, who use it for fern and flower gathering, etc.; geologists use it for collecting specimens, and ladies use it for fruit gathering.

The caul or wood basket (Fig. 173) may be described as an ordinary trug, only larger. It is from

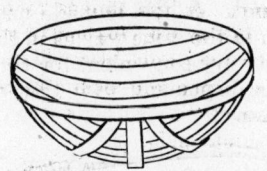

Fig. 174.—Stable or Feeding Basket.

3½ ft. to 5 ft. long; and as this would be a very unwieldy burden for anyone to carry, the handle is dispensed with, and instead a hand-hole is cut at each end, just under the rim (A, Fig. 173). It has a rim the same as an ordinary trug, and instead of the handle going over the top, it stops at the rim, to which it is nailed. There are two braces on each side of the handle, as shown. The laths thus are

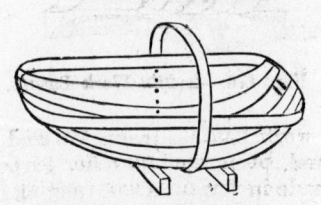

Fig. 175.—Coal Basket.

nailed in five different places, which makes it very strong and durable.

The stable or feeding basket (Fig. 174) is a form of trug used for feeding cattle and horses in their stables; it is believed to be used largely by the Army. It is made in the same way as the ordinary trug, except that it is quite round, and about 20 in. in diameter, the framework consisting of the rim and three braces, as illustrated.

The coal basket (Fig. 175) is very similar to the common trug, except that it is made smaller at one end than the other, and the handle is placed nearer to the wide end. A hole is made under the rim at the wide end, in the same way as in the caul basket. This makes it very convenient for throwing coal on the fire, thus dispensing with the ordinary coal-scuttle and shovel.

Fig. 176.—Lady's Work Basket.

Ladies' work baskets (Figs. 176 and 177) are in great demand, being used for other purposes as well. They are made in various sizes, ranging from 5 in. in diameter to 15 in., and are ornamented in various ways. The rims and handles are made on blocks in the same way as those of the ordinary trug, but, of course, more care must be taken with the work, and they must be made much lighter. The laths also must be shaved as thin as possible, and a good finish is given to the basket by fastening them together with upholsterers' silvered nails. After the laths are put in, they should be trimmed round, about ⅛ in. above the rim, and then small notches cut with the knife. This gives the basket an ornamental appearance at little expense of time. A good effect is also given by staining each alternate lath a different colour, the staining being done before the laths are nailed in. The baskets are much improved by having handles which fold down. This is effected by cutting the handle asunder, just above the rim, and inserting a piece of tin-plate 1 in. long, half of it in each part,

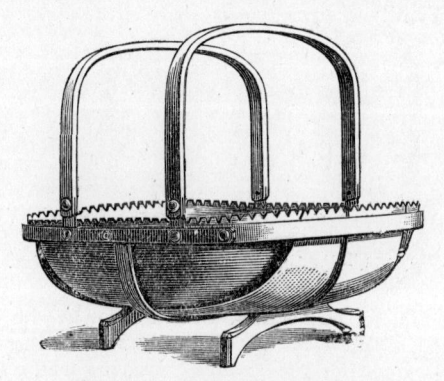

Fig. 177.—Lady's Work Basket.

with a rivet, formed with a tin tack or brad, through each, which forms a hinge for the handle, and allows it to fold easily. The hinge is made clear in the diagram, Fig. 178, in which B B are the pieces of tin-plate, and A A A A the rivets. Figs. 176 and 177 show baskets with one and two handles respectively.

The parcel-post basket has not so general a use as the other kinds of trugs, though for those who send game, fruit, etc., by parcel-post, it will be found useful. It is simply two ordinary baskets without handles, hung together at one end by the rims, so that, when folded together, they form a box. The rims can be tied together at the other end to make all secure. Its recommendation is its lightness, which saves postage, and its strength.

Handsome flower-pots can be made out of the same materials, and in the same way as the trugs. To make them, first cut out in ½-in. deal an octagon of the same size as the inside of the proposed flower-pot; this octagon will form the bottom of the pot. Make a rim of the same size or a shade larger inside measurement, and prepare eight laths, if a small pot, or sixteen, if a large one, and proceed to nail

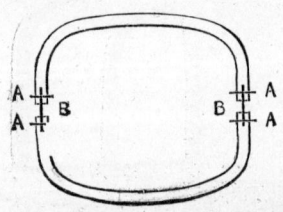

Fig. 178.—Folding Handles for Work Basket.

them, first to the bottom, and then to the rim, with silvered nails; trim off, and ornament in the same way as mentioned for ladies' work baskets. These pots can be used either as standing or hanging pots, and can be finished off with enamel paint.

Dolls' cradles can be made of the same materials, but the trug maker will now have gained such an experience that this and many other useful articles will suggest themselves to him; and there is no need to take up space in describing the process of making them. The same applies to the butcher's tray, which is exceedingly simple to make. It may be noted, however, in the case of the cradle, that if it is to rock, curved rockers must be put under the tray itself, instead of the straight pieces of wood that are generally added to it as feet.

CHAPTER XII.

MISCELLANEOUS BASKET WORK.

In this chapter attention will be devoted to a few of the jobs which occasionally the working basket maker has to undertake; and brief instructions will be given for making one or two kinds of baskets not yet mentioned.

For a hawker's oval basket with a false bottom, say 16 in. long, the basket being 9 in. deep, take eight rods, and tie a slarth of four lays of sticks, as illustrated in Figs. 57 to 59, pp. 56 and 57, and fill in the bottom by working rods in pairs, as described in Chapter V. When the bottom is finished, stake it, being particular to get a pair of stakes in the middle of both sides to form a space for the handle bow. After the stakes have been gathered and placed in a hoop, begin to upset with four rods, as described in Chapter V. After putting on two rounds of upsetting, weave in rods singly, as in Fig. 41, p. 39. If the space under the false bottom is to be utilised as well, a small opening must be left for a door, either at one of the ends or near a handle space. Each weaving rod is worked round the stake and back again until sufficient space D (Fig. 179) is left to admit or remove such articles as may be required. Of course, the door space D may require two or even three stakes left bare; only one is shown as an example. At about 4 in. from the border must be formed a ledge of some kind on which the false bottom rests. See that the weaving is of one depth all round; then take four fair-sized rods and work on a wale, as in Fig. 180. Place A behind stakes E, F, G; B behind F, G, H; C behind G, H, J, and D behind H, J, K; and repeat, each wale-rod passing in front of one stake and behind three; work them tight to form a substantial ledge for the false bottom.

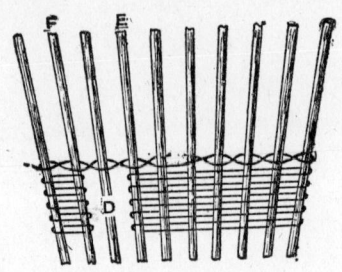

Fig. 179.—Weaving for Hawker's Basket.

Piece each wale-rod butt where it finishes, and lap the tops properly. Now finish weaving, and when the top wale is put round use four rods (see Fig. 43, p. 41). Work each rod inside two stakes and outside two stakes, piecing the butts as before. The border can now be laid down; this is worked much like the one in Fig. 46, p. 44, the difference being that

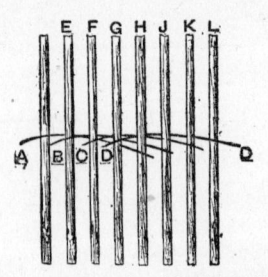

Fig. 180.—Waling for Hawker's Basket.

there are not any corners; instead, leave the space for the handle bow or bows exactly the same. A rod, cane, or skein handle, whichever is preferred, can be

MISCELLANEOUS BASKET WORK. 149

made, and for the last use three bows instead of two, as in Fig. 120, p. 111, and two scallom rods, as a more substantial handle will be required. The false bottom is made like the fixed one, and should fit well on the wale. The door can be formed with four scallom rods lapped on the stake E (Fig. 179), weaving between them sufficient small rods to cover the space to the stake F, and cramming the two outside ones beside each other. Cut off the second inside scallom, and cram the first down by the side of it. Cut

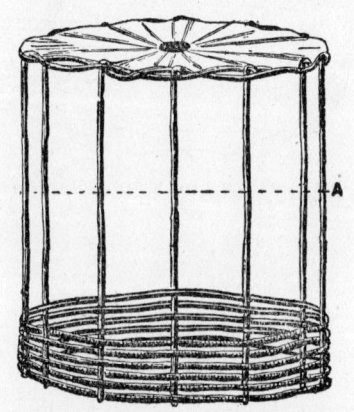

Fig. 181.—Basket for Show Fowls.

off the uncovered part of the stake in the space D, and fasten the door at the stake F in any convenient way. The four lapped parts of the scallom rods act as hinges on the stake E.

A round basket for conveying show fowls may be 2 ft. in diameter and 2 ft. or more in height, according to the size of the birds. The bottom is formed as in an ordinary basket or hamper, and the sides are as shown in Fig. 181. The wicker-work is made to a height of 6 in. at the base, and at the level A two well-twisted rods are put on as shown in plan (Fig.

182) for strength. The top is finished with two rods in a similar manner, and the upright rods are twisted, bent down, and worked in with the finishing rods so

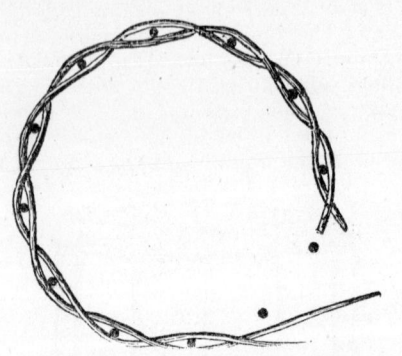

Fig. 182.—Woven Twisted Rods.

as to form a rim. The basket is lined with light canvas, which should project about 1 ft. above the top. The canvas is finished like a pillow-case, having a hem to receive a string; when this is drawn and tied there will remain a hole at the top which will give

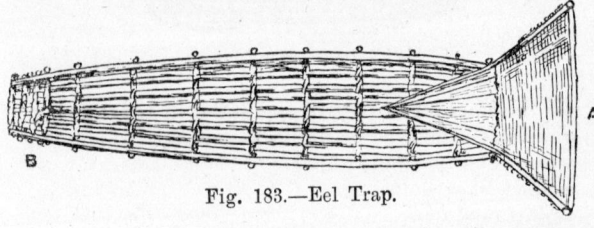

Fig. 183.—Eel Trap.

sufficient ventilation. These baskets are cheap, light, and quickly made.

Eel-traps for sinking in a river are made of wickerwork, as shown by Fig. 183. The body consists of a cigar-shaped basket about 3 ft. 6 in. long and about 6 in. diameter at the largest part. The sticks should be about ⅜ in. apart. At one end (A) a funnel-shaped basket is fitted up, the small end of which projects into the trap. This is made of pointed flexible wooden strips, which spring apart as the eels enter, but will not permit them to leave the trap. The opening B is used for putting in the bait and removing the captures, and is closed when the trap is in use with a piece of sacking tied over the mouth.

An easily made specimen of basket work is the

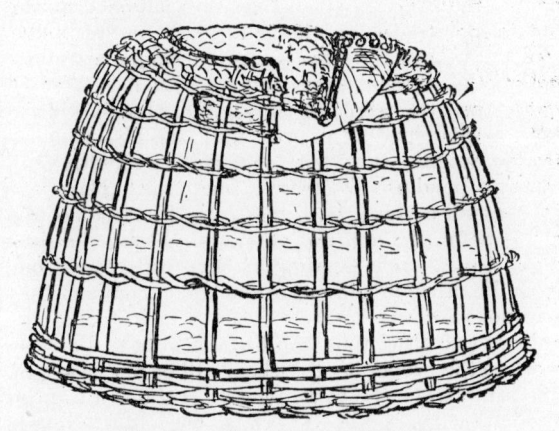

Fig. 184.—Crab and Lobster Pot.

crab and lobster pot, shown in Fig. 184. This is a mere openwork wicker basket, about 30 in. in diameter by 20 in. high, the bottom being made very strong. Stones are lashed to the bottom inside so as to cause the pot to sink, and a strong line having cork floats fixed at intervals to denote the position of the pot is attached to the side.

For making baskets or hand-guards for singlesticks, take about eight long thin osiers and with them form a slarth, as described on p. 49, and shown by Figs. 52 and 53. As both butts and tops of these eight osiers are to form the border, they must be laid thus—a butt, a top, a butt, and so on. Sse two small rods to tie the slarth. Four of the eight osiers will have to be laid first, then the other four across them. When the tie-rods have been worked alternately twice round, the osiers are opened in turn by working the tie-rods between them, thus forming sixteen uprights to receive the weaving, or pairing, as it is called. The half stick 1 (Fig. 52, p. 50) will not be required; a small piece is scalloped at the butt of one tie-rod and lapped round the four under rods. To get the hand-guard to shape, carefully gather the sixteen stakes and place them in a small hoop; peg the whole to the edge of the workboard with a small bodkin or wire nail passed through a leaden weight. Now form each stake by gently pulling and bending. Take two small rods, place one top behind a stake, with the tip end in front of the stake before it, and the other rod behind the next stake to the right; pair these two rods round one over the other in and out of the stakes. When they will not work any further, piece them with the butt ends of two other rods (see Fig, 40, p. 36). Pair the work to the proper depth, which will be between 3 in. and 4 in., when the stakes can be laid down to form the border, as in Fig. 185. A, B, and C first are laid down, each stake passing behind two others, in front of the third and fourth, and finishing in front of the sixth, as shown at F. The stakes D are to be laid down in turn. The fencing-stick is passed through near the border of one side of the guard, and out near the crown at the opposite side. Small wood pegs are put in the sticks outside to keep them in position.

Some instructions on repairing oval and square baskets may be given here.

Baskets should be repaired before they are too badly worn. As soon as the foot rim gets broken, well soak that part, draw out all foot stakes (with pincers, if necessary), and put on a new rim. If there is no foot rim, cut out the worn bottom with shears; or, if the bottom part is thoroughly soaked, the workman can push it inwards with his foot. If the bottom edge of the body itself is worn, pull off a few rounds, push down a stake wherever one may have

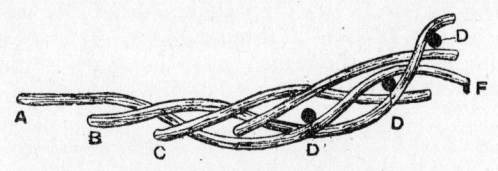

Fig. 185.—Border for Single-stick Hand-guard.

worn or broken, and work some upsetting (see Fig. 38, p. 35) to replace that which has been removed. A new bottom must be made to replace the old one. Of course, the stakes in the body must be cut quite level all round at the bend after the upsetting has been finished off. Occasionally gauge the bottom to the body so as to get a good fit; then cut off the ends of the bottom sticks, and tie in the bottom with osier bands. An oval basket will require about six bands, two at each side and one at each end. A large square basket may require eight or ten bands, three at each side and two at the ends. To keep the bottom in place while tying, push two or three bodkins

Fig. 186.—Tying-in Band.

through the upsetting and into the bottom, down beside the bottom sticks. Next pick out and point six or eight band rods. Push one down the upsetting in the body, and begin twisting it rope fashion from the tip end to the butt. The rod now can be drawn in and out exactly as can a piece of rope. With the bodkin, open the weaving in the bottom, about 4 in. from the edge, at the right-hand side of the nearest bottom stick; pull the band through from the inside, then out again at the other side of the same stick; twist it over the 4-in. lap twice, pulling it very tight and even, then carry it for about 6 in. up the side of the basket, and push it through to the left of a stake. Bring it out to the right about 1 in. nearer the bottom, and again twist it over itself three times along

Fig. 187.—Bottom of Strawberry Punnet.

the bottom twisted part; return it through the first loop, still keeping an even twist, then pass it through the edge of the bottom, and upset, again forming a close and even twist up the side; finally, pass it through the side loop, pull very tightly, and cut off the waste piece neat and close. Fig. 186 shows part of a tying-in band. A is passed through the side of the body and comes out again at the right-hand side of the stake, and is worked the whole length again, when it is turned in the loop in the bottom (outside), and finishes as at B, outside. The even twist is obtained by pulling tightly. When all the bands are finished, a foot rim can be worked on, as described

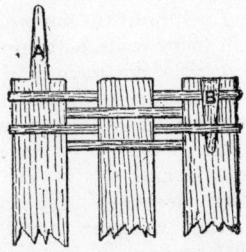

Fig. 188.—Uprights and Lacing of Strawberry Punnet.

on p. 45 in the chapter on making a grocer's basket. Should any of the top border stakes be broken, push down others in their places, bend them down, draw

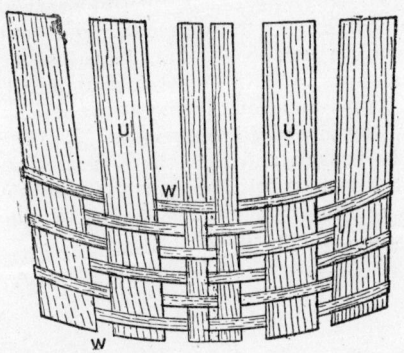

Fig. 189.—Uprights and Lacing of Strawberry Punnet.

them through from the front, and cram them, as shown in Fig. 47, p. 44. Some stakes will require merely pushing through the border from the front and cramming, the inside end being cut off close.

Strawberry punnets or baskets as used by fruiterers are made with thin strips of wood, well soaked before use. The bottom and uprights are comprised of six pieces of $\frac{1}{16}$ in. wood; the bottom and side pieces may be of ash, and the lacings, which are $\frac{1}{32}$ in. thick and $\frac{1}{4}$ in wide, may be of pine. To make a punnet $5\frac{1}{2}$ in. across the bottom and $2\frac{3}{4}$ in. deep, cross the six lengths (as shown in Fig. 187) under the left foot. Split A down half its length, which will give thirteen uprights. Take a $\frac{1}{4}$ in. lacing, put it between A and B, and weave it round to the right as shown between the split upright, and continue the weaving until the bottom is $5\frac{1}{2}$ in. wide. The cross pieces now are bent upwards carefully, and the tops held in a small hoop to keep them in position until a few rounds of the side lacings have been inserted, when the hoop can be dispensed with. As each length of lacing is finished, it is pieced with another (inside). When the depth is obtained, cut off level with the top every alternate ($2\frac{3}{4}$ in.) upright. Of the other uprights (only three are shown), a portion (A, Fig. 188) is shaved thin, bent outwards, and the ends tucked into the side as at B. Push in a long lacing at the left-hand side of one of the turned-down uprights. Lap one strand round the basket, and with the longest strand bind it and the last or top lacing firmly together. Fig. 189 is a section of a punnet body; w shows the lacings and u the uprights.

INDEX

Axe, Cleaving, 141
Awl, 15
Band on Doctor's Basket, 109
——, Tying-in, 154

Basket (*for details see under separate headings*)
—— Bottle-casings, 98-103
——, Brown Stain for, 15
——, Cane, 16-26, 112-131
——, Caul, 143
——, Coal, 144
——, Chemist's or Doctor's, 104-111
——, Fancy, 16-26, 112-131
——, Feeding, 143, 144
——, Flat Fruit, 64-73
——, Grocer's Square, 27-48
——, Ladies' Work, 144, 145
——, Linen, 55-63
——, Madeira Open-work, 130, 131
——, Mahogany Stain for, 15
——, Oblong Fancy, 117-121
——, Oval, 55-63
——, ——, Fancy, 24, 122
——, ——, for Hawker, 147-149
——, Parcel-post, 145, 146
——, Repairing, 152-155
——, Round, 49-54
——, ——, Fancy, 16-22
——, ——, for Show Fowls, 149, 150
——, Rubbish, 112, 113
——, Single-stick, 151-152
——, Square, 27-48
——, ——, Fancy, 117-121
——, Stable, 143, 144
——, Stains for, 15
——, Strawberry, 156
——, Sussex Trug (*see* Trug)
——, Walking-stick, 141-143
——, Wood, 143
Bedstead, Doll's, 129
Binding Fancy Handles, 120
Bleaching Cane, 15
Block, Screw, 9
——, ——, Use of, 27, 28
Boards for Trug Baskets, 140
——, Work, 14
Bodkins, 9
Border on Bottle-casing, 102
—— —— Doctor's Basket, 104-106
—— —— Flat Fruit Basket, 68, 69
—— —— Foot Rim of Elbow-chair, 83
—— —— Grocer's Basket, 41-43
—— —— Oval Linen Basket, 62
——, Plaited, 93, 94
—— on Round Basket, 53
—— round Elbow-chair Corner Posts, 84
—— on Single-stick Hand-guard, 152

Bottle-casing, Basket, 98-103
——, ——, Beginning, 98
——, ——, Border on, 102
——, ——, Cap of, 99
——, ——, Handle on, 102
——, ——, Slewing, 100, 101, 103
——, ——, Tap-opening in, 101
——, ——, Upsetting, 100
Bottom of Doctor's Basket, 104
——, False, to Oval Basket, 147, 148
—— of Flat Fruit Basket, 64
—— —— Grocer's Basket, 28-30
—— —— Oval Linen Basket, 55-58
—— —— Round Basket, 49-51
—— —— Trug Basket, 140
Bow for Basket Lid, 69-72
—— —— Doctor's Basket, 110, 111
—— —— Elbow-chair, 74-97
—— ——, ——, Lapping, 74
—— Handle of Grocer's Basket, 46, 47
—— ——, Lapping, 47
Boxwood Cleaves, 13
Bridge on Doctor's Basket, 106
Brown Stain for Baskets, 15
Buff-coloured Chairs, Osiers for, 13
Butcher's Tray, 145

Cane Baskets, 16-26, 112-131
——, Bleaching, 15
Casing, Bottle, 98-103
——, ——, Beginning, 98
——, ——, Border on, 102
——, ——, Cap of, 99
——, ——, Handle on, 102
——, ——, Slewing, 100, 101, 103
——, ——, Tap-opening in, 101
——, ——, Upsetting, 100
Caul Trug Basket, 143
Chair, Buff-coloured, Osiers for, 13
——, Doll's Garden, 122
——, Plain, 129, 130
——, Round, 123
——, Wicker Elbow, 74-97 (*see also* Elbow-chair)
Chemist's Basket, 104-111
——, Border on, 104-106
——, Bottom of, 104
——, Bow for, 110, 111
——, Bridge on, 106
——, Flap Lids of, 106
——, Handle for, 110, 111
——, Lapping Handle of, 110
——, Staples for, 111
——, Twist or Band on, 109
——, Tying on Lids of, 109
——, Upsetting, 105
——, Wale on, 105
Chip, Plaited, 113
Cleave, Boxwood Splitting, 13

BASKET WORK.

Cleave for Peeling Osiers, 10
——, Splitting, Making Skeins with, 13, 14, 95-97
Cleaving Wood for Trug Baskets, 140
Cleaving-axe, 141
Coal Basket, 144
Cob, 49-54
——, Border for, 53
——, Bottom of, 49-51
——, Laying Slarth for, 49-51
——, Slewing for, 50, 53
——, Staking Bottom of, 51
——, Upsetting Stakes of, 51, 52
——, White Randed, 54
Commander, 9
Corner Posts, Elbow-chair, 84-86, 92, 93
——, ——, Bordering Round, 84
——, ——, Plaiting over, 97
Crab and Lobster Pot, 151
Cradle, Doll's, 124, 146
Cramming, 45

Damping Osiers, 12
Doctor's Basket, 104-111
—— ——, Border on, 104-106
—— ——, Bottom of, 104
—— ——, Bow for, 110, 111
—— ——, Bridge on, 106
—— ——, Flap Lids of, 106
—— ——, Handle for, 110, 111
—— ——, Lapping Handle of, 110
—— ——, Staples for, 111
—— ——, Twist or Band on, 109
—— ——, Tying on Lids of, 109
—— ——, Upsetting, 105
—— ——, Wale on, 105
Doll's Bedstead, 129
—— Cradle, 124, 146
—— Garden Chair, 122
—— Plain Chair, 129, 130
—— Round Chair, 123
—— Sofa, 129
—— Table, 124-126
Drawing-knife, 132
Draw-shave, 132

Edging (see also Border)
——, Rope, 25
——, Trellis-work, 21
Eel Traps, 150, 151
Elbow-chair, 74-97
——, Back of, 86-88
——, Bordering Foot Rim of, 83
——, —— round Corner Post of, 84
——, Bow for, 74
——, By-staking, 88
——, Corner Posts of, 84-86, 91, 93
——, "Fetching," 80-83, 88-92
——, Foot of, 77
——, Height of, 77
——, Lapping Bow of, 74
——, Open-work on, 80
——, Plaited Border on, 93, 94

Elbow-chair, Plaiting Corner Posts of, 97
——, Seat of, 76, 77
——, Skeins for Posts of, 95-97
——, Staking, 74, 75, 78
——, Upsetting, 79
——, Weaving on, 74-76
Fancy (see also Doll's)
—— Basket, Binding, 116
—— —— Lid, 117
—— Furniture, 122-126, 129, 14
—— Madeira Basket, 130, 131
—— Oblong Baskets, 117-121
—— Oval Basket, 24, 122
—— Round Basket, 16-22
—— Rubbish Basket, 112, 113
—— Square Baskets, 117-121
Feeding Basket, 143, 144
Feet of Trug Basket, 141
"Fetching" on Elbow-chair, 80-83, 88-92
Fire-screen, 126, 127
Flap Lids on Doctor's Basket, 106
Flat Basket (see Fruit Basket)
—— Iron, 10, 30
—— Pulp or Insides, 113
Flower-pots, 146
Foot Rim of Elbow-chair, 77
—— —— Grocer's Basket, 45
Fowls, Round Basket for, 149, 150
Fruit Basket, 64-73
——, Border on, 68, 69
——, Bottom of, 64
——, Bow for Lid of, 69-72
——, Handles on, 66, 67
——, Lid of, 70-73
——, Pairing off in making, 68
——, Tying on Lid of, 72, 73
——, Upsetting Sides of, 64-66
——, Weaving on, 66
Furniture, Doll's, 122-126, 129, 146

Garden Chair, Doll's, 122
Grease-horn, 32
Green Rush Plait, 113
Grocer's Basket, 27-48
——, Beginning, 28
——, Bordering on, 41-43
——, Bottom of, 28-30
——, Bow Handle of, 46, 47
——, Foot Rim on, 45
——, Hooping Stakes of, 33, 34
——, Lapping Handle of, 47
——, Picking, 45
——, Randing on, 37-40
——, Stakes for, 31
——, Staking Bottom of, 31-34
——, Strainers for, 38
——, Upsetting Rim Stakes of, 46
——, —— Sides of, 34-37
——, Wale on, 40, 41
——, Weaving on, 36, 37-40

Hampers, Handles for, 67

INDEX. 159

Hand-guards, Single-stick, 151-152
Handles on Bottle-casings, 102
——— Doctor's Baskets, 110, 111
———, Fancy, 120
——— on Flat Fruit Baskets, 66, 67
——— Grocer's Baskets, 46, 47
——— Hampers, 67
———, Lapping, 47
——— on Oval Linen Basket, 62, 63
——— Round Baskets, 26
——— Trug Baskets, 139
Hawker's Oval Basket, 147-149
Hooping Stakes, 33, 34
Horn, Grease, 32
Horse, Shaving, 132-134

Insides or Flat Pulp, 113
Iron Commander, 9
———, Flat, 10, 30

Jar-casing (*see* Bottle-casing)
Joints in Weaving, 18

Knife, Drawing, 132
———, Picking, 9
———, ———, Sharpening, 45
———, Shop, 9
———, Trimming, 9

Lacing Strawberry Punnet, 156
Ladies' Work Baskets, 144, 145
Lapping Bow of Elbow-chair, 74
——— Handles, 47
——— Handle of Doctor's Basket, 110
Lids on Doctor's Basket, 106
——— Fancy Baskets, 117
——— Flat Fruit Baskets, 70-73
Linen Basket, 55-63
———, Border on, 62
———, Bottom of, 55-58
———, Handles on, 62-63
———, Randing on, 61
———, Slarth for, 55-58
———, Staking Bottom of, 59
———, Upsetting Sides of, 59, 60
———, Wale on, 61
Lobster Pot, 151

Madeira Open-work Basket, 130, 131
Mahogany Stain for Baskets, 15
Measure, Yard, 10
Materials, 15, 113, 116, 140

Newspaper Rack, 127-129

Oblong Fancy Baskets, 117-121
——— ———, Binding Handles of, 120
——— ———, Handles for, 120
——— ———, Weaving on, 119-120
Open-work Basket, Madeira, 130, 131
——— or Elbow-chair, 80
Open-work Patterns, 113, 114

Open-work, Crossed, 114
Osiers, Boiling, 13
———, for Buff-coloured Chairs, 13
———, Cleave for Peeling, 10
———, ——— Splitting, 13
———, Damping, 11
———, Making Skeins from, 13, 14, 97
———, Obtaining, 10
———, Peeling, 10, 11
———, Shears for Cutting, 9, 10
———, Splitting, 95
Oval Basket, 55-63
——— ———, Border on, 62
——— ———, Bottom of, 55-58
——— ———, Handles on, 62, 63
——— ———, Hawker's, 147-149
——— ———, Randing on, 61
——— ———, Repairing, 152-155
——— ———, Slarth for, 55-58
——— ———, Staking Bottom of, 59
——— ———, Upsetting Sides of, 59, 60
——— ———, Wale on, 61
——— Fancy Basket, 24

Pairing-off in making Flat Basket, 68
Paper Rack, 127-129
Parcel-post Baskets, 145, 146
Peeling Osiers, 10, 11
Picking Grocer's Basket, 45
Picking-knife, 9
———, Sharpening, 45
Pink-tie, 116
Plait, Green Rush, 113
——— on Madeira Basket, 131
———, Straw Woven, 113
Plaited Border, 93, 94
——— Chip, 113
Posts, Elbow-chair, 84-86, 92, 93
———, ———, Bordering round, 84
———, ———, Plaiting over, 97
Pot, Crab and Lobster, 151
———, Eel, 150, 151
Pulp, Flat, 113
Punnet, Strawberry, 156

Rack, Paper, 127-129
Randed Cobs, 54
Randing (*see also* Weaving)
——— on Grocer's Basket, 37-40
——— ——— Oval Linen Basket, 61
Repairing Baskets, 152-155
Rim, Foot, of Elbow-chair, 77
———, ———, ——— Grocer's Basket, 45
——— Stakes, Upsetting, 46
——— for Trug Basket, 139
Rope Edging, 25
Round Basket, 49-54
———, Border for, 53
———, Bottom of, 49-51
———, Laying Slarth for, 49-51
——— for Show Fowls, 149, 150
———, Slewing for, 50, 53
———, Staking Bottom of, 51
———, Upsetting Stakes of, 51, 52

Round Chair, Doll's, 123
—— Cob (see Cob)
—— Fancy Basket, 16-22
Rubbish Basket, 112, 113
—— ——, Weaving on, 112, 113
Rush Plait, Green, 113

Screen, Fire, 126, 127
Screw-block, 9
——, Using, 27, 28
Seat of Elbow-chair, 76, 77
Sharpening Picking-knife, 45
Shave, 13
——, Draw, 132
——, Upright, 14
Shaving-brake, 135
Shaving-horse, 132-134
Shears, 9, 10
Shop Knife, 9
Single-stick Hand-guards, 151-152
Skeins, Making, 13, 14, 95-97
Slarth for Oval Linen Basket, 55-58
—— Round Basket, 49-51
Slewing, 50, 53
—— Basket-casing, 100, 101, 103
Sofa, Doll's, 129
Splitting Osiers, 95
——, Cleave for, 13
Square Basket, Grocer's (see Grocer's)
——, Repairing, 152-155
—— Fancy Baskets, 117-121
—— ——, Binding Handles of, 120
—— ——, Handles for, 120
—— ——, Weaving on, 119, 120
Stable Basket, 143, 144
Stains for Baskets, 15
Stakes for Grocer's Basket, 31
——, Hooping, 33, 34
Staking Bottom of Grocer's Basket, 31-34
—— —— Oval Linen Basket, 59
—— —— Round Basket, 51
—— Elbow-chair, 74, 75, 78
Staples, 111
Steam Trough, 135-138
Steaming Wood, 135-138
Strainers, 38
Strawberry Punnet, 156
Straw-woven Plait, 113
Sussex Trug Baskets, 132-146 (see also Trug Baskets)

Table, Doll's, 124-126
Tap Opening in Bottle Casing, 101
Tools, 9-15, 132-135, 141
Trap, Crab and Lobster, 151
——, Eel, 150, 151
Tray, Butcher's, 146
Trellis-work Edging, 21
Trimming-knife, 9
Trough, Steam, 135-138
Trug Baskets, 132-146
—— ——, Boards for 140

Trug Baskets, Bottoms of, 140
——, Caul, 143
——, Cleaving Wood for, 140
——, Cleaving-axe for making, 141
——, Coal, 144
——, Doll's Cradle, 146
——, Drawing-knife for making, 132
——, Feeding, 143, 144
——, Feet for, 141
——, Flower-pot, 146
——, Handles for, 139
——, Ladies' Work, 144, 145
——, Parcel-post, 145, 146
——, Putting together, 139, 140
——, Rims for, 139
——, Shaving-brake for making, 135
——, Shaving-horse for making, 132-134
——, Stable, 143, 144
——, Steaming Wood for, 135-138
——, Tools for making, 132-135, 141
——, Walking-stick, 141-143
——, Wood, 143
Twist on Doctor's Basket, 109
Tying-in Band, 154
Tying-on Lids of Doctor's Baskets, 109
—— —— Flat Fruit Baskets, 72, 73

Upright Shave, 14
Upsetting Bottle-casing, 100
—— Doctor's Basket, 105
—— Elbow-chair, 79
—— Fruit Basket, 64-66
—— Grocer's Basket, 34-37
—— Oval Linen Basket, 59, 60
—— Rim Stakes, 46
—— Round Basket, 51, 52
—— Square Basket, 34-37

Wale on Doctor's Basket, 105
—— —— Grocer's Basket, 40, 41
—— —— Hawker's Basket, 147
—— —— Oval Linen Basket, 61
Walking-stick Trug Baskets, 141-143
Weaving (see also Randing)
—— on Elbow-chair, 74-76
—— —— Flat Fruit Basket 66
—— —— Hawker's Basket, 147
——, Joints in, 18
——, Simple, 30
—— on Square Fancy Baskets, 119, 120
Wetting Osiers, 12
Wicker Elbow-chair (see Elbow-chair)
Wood Basket, 143
Work Baskets, Ladies', 144, 145
Work-boards, 14

Yard-measure, 10

Zig-zag Pattern, 115

PRINTED BY CASSELL & COMPANY, LIMITED, LUDGATE HILL, LONDON, E.C.
10.1208

HANDICRAFT SERIES (continued).

Electro-Plating. With Numerous Engravings and Diagrams.
Contents.—Introduction. Tanks, Vats, and other Apparatus. Batteries, Dynamos, and Electrical Accessories. Appliances for Preparing and Finishing Work. Silver-Plating, Copper-Plating. Gold-Plating. Nickel-Plating and Cycle-Plating. Finishing Electro-Plated Goods. Electro-Plating with Various Metals and Alloys. Index.

Clay Modelling and Plaster Casting. With 153 Engravings and Diagrams.

Violins and Other Stringed Instruments. With about 180 Illustrations.
Contents.—Materials and Tools for Violin Making. Violin Moulds. Violin Making. Varnishing and Finishing Violins. Double Bass and a Violoncello. Japanese One-string Violin. Mandolin Making. Guitar Making. Banjo Making. Zither Making. Dulcimer Making. Index.

Glass Writing, Embossing, and Fascia Work. (Including the Making and Fixing of Wood Letters and Illuminated Signs.) With 129 Illustrations.
Contents.—Plain Lettering and Simple Tablets. Gold Lettering. Blocked Letters. Stencil Cutting. Gold Etching. Embossing. French or Treble Embossing. Incised Fascias, Stall-plates, and Grained Background. Letters in Perspective; Spacing Letters. Arrangement of Wording and Colors. Wood Letters. Illuminated Signs. Temporary Signs for Windows. Imitation Inlaid Signs. Imitation Mosaic Signs. Specimen Alphabets. Index.

Photographic Chemistry. With 31 Engravings and Diagrams.

Photographic Studios and Dark Rooms. With 180 Illustrations.
Contents.—Planning Studios. Building Studios. Portable and Temporary Studios. Studios Improvised from Greenhouses, Dwelling Rooms, etc. Lighting of Studios. Backgrounds. Scenic Accessories. Dark-Rooms. Portable Dark-Rooms. Dark-Room Fittings. Portable Dark Tent. Index.

Motor Bicycle Building. With 137 Illustrations and Diagrams.
Contents.—Frame for Motor Bicycle. Patterns for Frame Castings. Building Frame from Castings. Making 3½ H. P. Petrol Motor. Spray Carburettor for 3½ H. P. Motor. Ignition Coils for Motor Cycles. Light-weight Petrol Motor for Attachment to Roadster Bicycle. Spray Carburettor for Light-weight Motor. Index.

Rustic Carpentry. With 172 Illustrations.
Contents.—Light Rustic Work, Flower Stands, Vases, etc. Tables, Chairs and Seats. Gates and Fences. Rosery Work, Porch, Swing Canopy Aviary, Footbridges Verandahs. Tool Houses, Garden Shelters, etc. Summer Houses, Dovecot. Index.

Pumps and Rams: Their Action and Construction. With 171 Illustrations.
Contents.—Suction Pumps and Lift Pumps. Making Simple Suction Pumps. Pump Cup Leathers, Pump Valves, Ram or Plunger Pumps. Making Bucket and Plunger Pump. Construction of Plumbers' Force Pump, Wooden Pumps, Small Pumps for Special Purposes, Centrifugal Pumps, Air Lift, Mammoth, and Pulsometer Pumps, Hydraulic Rams. Index.

Domestic Jobbing. With 107 Illustrations.
Contents.—Cutlery Grinding, Sharpening and Repairing. Simple Soldering and Brazing. China Riveting and Repairing. Chair Caning, Furniture Repairing, Glazing Windows, Umbrella Making and Repairing. Index.

Tinplate Work. With 280 Illustrations and Diagrams.
Contents.—Tinmen's Tools, Appliances and Materials. Elementary Examples in Tinplate. Hollowing Tinplate. Simple Round Articles in Tinplate. Saucepan Making. Square and Oval Kettle Making. Oil Cooking Stove. Set of Workshop Oil Cans. Fancy Paste Cutters. Lamps and Lanterns. Index.

Other Volumes in Preparation.

DAVID McKAY, Publisher, 610 South Washington Square, Philadelphia.

TECHNICAL INSTRUCTION.

Important New Series of Practical Volumes. Edited by PAUL N. HASLUCK. With numerous Illustrations in the Text. Each book contains about 160 pages, crown 8vo. Cloth, $1.00 each, postpaid.

Practical Draughtsmen's Work. With 226 Illustrations.
Contents.—Drawing Boards. Paper and Mounting. Draughtsmen's Instruments. Drawing Straight Lines. Drawing Circular Lines. Elliptical Curves. Projection. Back Lining Drawings. Scale Drawings and Maps. Colouring Drawings. Making a Drawing. Index.

Practical Gasfitting. With 120 Illustrations.
Contents.—How Coal Gas is Made. Coal Gas from the Retort to the Gas Holder. Gas Supply from Gas Holder to Meter. Laying the Gas Pipe in the House. Gas Meters. Gas Burners. Incandescent Lights. Gas Fittings in Workshops and Theatres. Gas Fittings for Festival Illuminations. Gas Fires and Cooking Stoves. Index.

Practical Staircase Joinery. With 215 Illustrations.
Contents.—Introduction: Explanation of Terms. Simple Form of Staircase—Housed String Stair: Measuring, Planning, and Setting Out. Two-flight Staircase. Staircase with Winders at Bottom. Staircase with Winders at Top and Bottom. Staircase with Half-space of Winders. Staircase over an Oblique Plan. Staircase with Open or Cut Strings. Cut String Staircase with Brackets. Open String Staircase with Bull-nose Step. Geometrical Staircases. Winding Staircases. Ships' Staircases. Index.

Practical Metal Plate Work. With 247 Illustrations.
Contents.—Materials used in Metal Plate Work. Geometrical Construction of Plane Figures. Geometrical Construction and Development of Solid Figures. Tools and Appliances used in Metal Plate Work. Soldering and Brazing. Tinning. Re-tinning and Galvanising. Examples of Practical Metal Plate Work. Examples of Practical Pattern Drawing. Index.

Practical Graining and Marbling. With 79 Illustrations.
Contents.—Graining: Introduction, Tools, and Mechanical Aids. Graining Grounds and Graining Colors. Oak Graining in Oil. Oak Graining in Spirit and Water Colours. Pollard Oak and Knotted Oak Graining. Maple Graining Mahogany and Pitch-pine Graining. Walnut Graining. Fancy Wood Graining. Furniture Graining. Imitating Woods by Staining. Imitating Inlaid Woods. Marbling: Introduction, Tools, and Materials. Imitating Varieties of Marble. Index.

Painters' Oils Colors and Varnishes. With Numerous Illustrations.
Contents.—Painters' Oils. Color and Pigments. White Pigments. Blue Pigments. Chrome Pigments. Lake Pigments. Green Pigments. Red Pigments. Brown and Black Pigments. Yellow and Orange Pigments. Bronze Colors. Driers. Paint Grinding and Mixing. Gums, Oils, and Solvents for Varnishes. Varnish Manufacture. Index.

Practical Plumbers' Work. With 298 Illustrations.
Contents.—Materials and Tools Used. Solder and How to Make It. Sheet Lead Working. Pipe Bending. Pipe Jointing. Lead Burning. Lead-Work on Roofs. Index.

Practical Pattern Making. With 295 Illustrations.
Contents.—Foundry Patterns and Foundry Practice. Jointing-up Patterns. Finishing Patterns. Circular Patterns. Making Core Boxes. Boring Holes in Castings. Patterns and Moulds for Iron Columns. Steam-Engine Cylinder Patterns and Core Boxes. Worm Wheel Pattern. Lathe Bed Patterns. Head Stock and Poppet Patterns. Slide-rest Patterns. Valve Patterns and Core Boxes. Index.

Practical Handrailing. With 144 Illustrations.
Contents.—Principles of Handrailing. Definition of Terms. Geometrical Drawing. Simple Handrails. Wreathed Handrails on the Cylindrical System. The Uses of Models. Obtaining Tangents and Bevels. Face Moulds: their Construction and Use. Twisting the Wreath. Completing the Handrail. Orthogonal or Right-angle System of Setting Wreathed Handrails. Handrails for Stone Stairs. Setting out Scrolls for Handrails. Setting out Moulded Caps. Intersecting Handrails without Basements. Index.